£11·95

Beauty
and the
Priest

By
Rev. Patrick McNamara
Formerly "Father Pat"

OZARK
MOUNTAIN
PUBLISHERS
P.O. Box 754
Huntsville, AR 72740-0754

For permission, or serialization, condensation, adaptions, or for our catalog of other publications, write to Ozark Mountain Publishers, P.O. Box 754, Huntsville, AR 72740-0754, Attn.: Permission Department.

Library of Congress Cataloging-in-Publication Data
Patrick McNamara, 1950–
   Beauty and the Priest by Rev. Patrick McNamara
   Former Roman Catholic priest combines organized religious teachings with New Age/Metaphysical teachings.
1. Religion 2. Metaphysics 3. Spirituality
I. McNamara, Rev. Patrick, 1950– II. Title
Library of Congress Catalog Card Number: 97-066769
ISBN: 1-886940-01-0

Cover Design: Jenelle Johannes
Book set in Caxton, Linotext & Cortez typefaces.
Book Design: Kris Kleeberg
Photo Preparation: Richard Thompson

Published by:

OZARK
MOUNTAIN
PUBLISHERS
P.O. Box 754
Huntsville, AR 72740-0754
Printed in the United States of America

Dedicated To Beauty

... and may you all find the many
exquisite ways God has created
Beauty in your lives.

Table of Contents

ACKNOWLEDGMENTS

I would like to acknowledge all of the "angels in skins" who have stood by me, walked and adventured with me, and gave me that gentle push when I needed it.

To my mother and father and supportive family.

To my kindred spirits on the edges of new horizons of God: Adele Tinning, Elisabeth Kübler-Ross, Sarita and Miguel, Claire O'Classen, Nancy and Neale Walsch, and Jacque Snyder.

A heart-felt thanks to my play friends in Spirit: Joe Bravo; The Gang: Rob, Chris K, Rod, Chris S, Irv and Al, Kathy O, Jeff (you must be smiling up there!), Rick and Shelley—"my buds" ... and so many more.

To my "families away from family": Aunt Margaret, the Mortons, Elbecks Gambelins, and Treglias. To Margaret and Buddy and all the Alvarez's who got me through my infancy years of priesthood (and with me in so many other journeys).

Love and thanksgiving to my catholic community and especially to my brother priests and their friendship: Scottie and Peter E.

To my spiritual companion, Joshua, a.k.a Jesus ... for your patience and persistence.

To all those who helped put together and edit this book and get it to the presses: Larry and Connie Sheehan, Noelle Denke (and the support of the entire staff at *The Light Connection* newspaper—tlcnews.com) and most of all to Dolores Cannon and Ozark Mountain Publishing for their faith in this book.

And I am eternally grateful to the love of my life, whose angelic wings touched my light and awakened my heart to experience a greater playground of God, my Beauty, Colleen Anderson.

Introduction

Have you ever seen a man put his entire hand into another's stomach and remove cancerous tissues? *I have!*

Can you imagine going to a funeral and peering into the coffin and seeing none other than you? *Preside over your own funeral and it will save your life!*

Do you believe you have lived here before? *God does! I know I have and it has changed my life.*

Have you ever really, truly, forgiven yourself? Totally let go of guilt and shame? Ready to live in the eternal moment of now? *It is possible. I did and I do!*

Would you like to know why a priest left the church with trust and confidence to fall in love with the love of his life? *I will tell you that story.*

Do you think you can ever release your fears of hell, judgment and damnation? *I have learned a way!*

Could you ever conceive that Jesus would stand right before you and speak directly to you? *He did so with me and continues to dialogue with me daily.*

Have you ever secretly desired to know more about God than has been told you by your church? I know the answers are available!

These are just a few of the grand adventures I explored to find out more about God in the New Age. If you dare to read the following pages, you will find yourself receiving answers to questions that you have longed to ask for many a year. If you have chosen to remain an active member of an orthodox religion, these journeys will empower you to love and challenge that church. For those of you who have moved beyond religion into new horizons, these wisdoms will be most reaffirming that you have moved in the right direction.

God is "in there," in the church, in more ways than have been told you. God is "out there," in the New Age movement, in more ways than you can imagine. Be a part of this great and gracious God, for in finding God, you will surely find yourself.

Preface

"On his way to Damascus, as he came near the city,
suddenly a light from the sky flashed around him.
He fell to the ground and heard a voice saying to him,
"Saul, Saul! Why do you persecute me?"
"Who are you, Lord?" he asked.
"I am Jesus, whom you persecute," the voice said.
"But get up and go into the city,
where you will be told what you must do."
Acts 9:3–6 **The Conversion of St. Paul**

here do YOU usually get **your** inspirational thoughts or moments? At a sunset? Over a candlelight dinner? While walking in the woods? Kneeling at prayer in church? Deep in meditation? In the shower? Say what? … in the shower? Well, that is where I heard my gentle-voiced Lord speak thus to me: "Why don't you write a book based on the question, 'How do you do it, Father?' " Gee whizz, God, couldn't you be a bit stronger in letting me know the message was really from you? After all, St. Paul was knocked to the ground, blinded by the light and couldn't speak for some time. But, then again, "You're right God, I really don't want to be hit in a car accident and have a blinding message delivered to me while I'm in the hospital, deep in a coma. The shower will do!"

That is where it all started for me. I have asked several friends where they get inspirational ideas. I've found out that I'm not so much in outer limits compared to other people. This survey of others is just an affirmation of the many new and innovative ideas I receive in the morning. But this idea, to write a book, was a very bold one and a little bit scary. I immediately called my friend and co-adventurer searching new horizons, and she said, "Go for it! There are many people out there who would benefit from such a book about how a Catholic can feel comfortable in the New Age."

The thoughts and ideas began to pour forth. I was excited and ecstatic and felt as though I had regained another level of motivation to help work for the Kingdom. Beauty! Beautiful! These were two words I continued to hear buzzing in my ears. Beauty ... there is more Beauty to be encountered beyond the four walls of the church. Beautiful ... life is meant to be beautiful, not a drudgery filled with fear and the unknown. The Beauty of God could be found and seen in so many new and exciting ways. (You will notice that Beauty, throughout this book, will have a capital "B." "B"eauty, like Truth, Wisdom, *etc.*, represents God. "B"eauty is also the love of my life. I am sure you can tell the difference ... although, most of the time I can't!)

But ... just like clockwork ... that good old guilt and fear began to rear its ugly head. What would the church think of this book? What will I say to the Bishop when he calls me in and asks, "What's all this stuff on channeling and reincarnation?" How will I be able to convince people of the truth and reality of psychic surgery? My mind continued to race, "But what about ... what about? ? ?"

"Whoa, Patrick! Wait just a minute! Who gave you this idea in the first place?," chided that gentle voice within. I began to realize that if God had directed me to write this book, then I would have to trust and have confidence in the messages and be a valiant messenger. Phew, I got over that speed bump in my Spiritual life. Now I just have to remember what that gentle voice within said, so that when I hit the next bump, I'll be ready.

The next bump? Here it comes: what happens if I leave the priesthood while writing this book or sometime after? WOULD PEOPLE STILL READ THE BOOK? Would they listen to these new stories of Beauty if I didn't have "the collar" to back them up? I have (had, I should now say) no intentions of leaving the priesthood. Although when the going gets tough (as it often does when people are too critical, stuck in old ways or too nosy about my private life), I do wonder how Jesus persevered and made it. Aren't there other ways, just as valid as the priesthood, to work for the Kingdom? After ruminating all these thoughts back and forth across the walls of my mind, I came to a screeching conclusion: **This book has been directed by the Father in heaven and is for my Father in heaven.** Therefore, my God, in all of God's beautiful, magnificent way, will take care of reaching the people that need to be touched by this particular message whether I stay in the priesthood or not. Yes, it is interesting that a **Catholic priest**, is espousing these new and different ideas. I was a priest in the Catholic Church for fourteen years! But the thrust of the messages in this book are from God, and the purpose of them is to broaden **our** horizons and open **our** eyes to new ways of seeing God in **our** world. It is because of **the message**, not the messenger, that this book will make the Kingdom of God a greater reality on earth as equally as it is in heaven. And, as you will find out in the turning of these pages, I, too, experience this beautiful Kingdom of God beyond the priesthood.

Speed Bump Number Three: My conscious mind told me, "This is blasphemy! How can you even attempt to write such nonsense?" I admit that some of what I say seems to go against what you have been led to believe. However, it is my contention that these subjects are new branches that can be explored from the same tree, grounded in the same roots of God, the Creator. "Parts are parts," as they say. A tree is a tree. Beauty is Beauty. As will be explained in the forthcoming chapters, I think you will see that the areas being explored in the New Age are not so foreign to our church and the ways of our brother Jesus, who taught the ways of God so many years ago.

May the peace and love of Christ reside deeply within you as you open your mind and heart to what is in these pages. *Shalom.*

A Caveat

Buckle up your seat belts! In order to find God, to find Beauty in new ways, to actually break on through to the other side of your formal religious training, you have to expect some rough terrain. Many readers of this book will have ingrained in their minds traditional dogmas and belief systems which you have been told not to "toy with." So in order to expand your mind, to "open new windows" (quoting our old friend Pope John XXIII), to allow the ever-present, living Spirit of God to rush in and through your life, you are going to have to let yourself explore new territory, break new ground and reach for new stars.

Numerous attempts will be made to make you feel comfortable along the journey by using familiar language. Often times God will still be called *Father*. This may make some feel they are being thrown back to the middle ages with the concept of an old man on a throne judging you all to … whatever. Some, on the other hand, feel very comforted by this concept of a good, gentle father-type always looking over his children with care and concern. Attempts will be made to help you see that God is more than a father, a mother and is not only both but is All That Is. **BUT,** just as often, you may feel very *uncomfortable* and even lost in a foreign land, when taboo subjects come up such as reincarnation, channeling, psychic surgery and much more.

Many of you will have already proceeded with courage into these areas and the lay of the land will not look so strange. Therefore, some preflight instructions, if you will.

First of all, keep an open mind. That is your God-given right: to think freely and observe all that is around you; think and *then* come to a conclusion. If you rush to judgment or attempt to pigeonhole what you are about to read with long words like "pantheism," "heresy," "iconoclast" or "trans-whatever," you may miss some important angles through which God attempts to shine. Secondly, FEEL! I remember some advice I was given once when told how better to listen to the Gospels read during Mass. I was told that it was best to place yourself right there and _"experience and feel"_ what was going on. Be an active player in the scheme of things. In doing so, I, myself, have had some very profound moments while listening to the Gospels and "being" there. I have felt Jesus speak his messages of truth directly to me. I have experienced the dryness of the desert, the tempestuous storm on the Sea of Galilee, the sadness of watching a friend die on a cross and the ecstatic renewal and joy of experiencing that friend in a new life form. These "being there" moments helped the message sink deeper into my psyche and have spurred me on to live the message out in truth.

Therefore, *BE THERE* as you read this book. As I begin to tell about the excitement of having lunch with Elisabeth Kübler-Ross, **feel** yourself sitting across from her. When I sit down at the table across from Adele Tinning and the energy in the table starts to vibrate and raise the table, **imagine** that same energy there with you. You are safe, you are light, you are love and only goodness follows you through these stories. When I venture to the ruins in Mexico and climb the Pyramid of the Sun or enter into "heaven" and stand before the Portal of the Masters, **feel** the exhilaration and adrenaline course through your veins. As I feel the helping power of God channeled through the hands of the foremost psychic surgeon, Alex Orbito, radiate through my body, **feel** your body accepting God's love and perfect health for you. Imagination and beliefs are the doorway to and through God. **Believe** all of this for yourself, too. Join me as we sit around the sacred fire in Manitoba and **sense** the Grandfather and Grandmother Spirits blessing us. **Be touched** by my wolf-clan Spirit guides as they nuzzle their warm noses under my chin and urge me on my path as a warrior. **Stand strong** with me as the Indian warriors passionately plea for the "white man" to honor the earth, its teachings and all its valuable heritage.

Most of all, **celebrate the love** that is shared as the story of the Priest finding his real Beauty. Love is God ... God is love. If you are not presently in love, act as though you are when you read this chapter. The mind will not know the difference. Your heart **will experience** the difference love makes in one's life. Then, in all its magical, mystical ways, you will draw it into your own life.

Although the road may seem bumpy at times when you read these adventures, your belts are secure. There are many angels and guides who lead you to read this book. Continuing to call on these helpers will allow you to move easily through any obstacles you may encounter. The 23rd Psalm indeed says, "Only goodness and kindness shall follow you all the days of your life and you shall live in the house of the Lord for years to come." Because you have been drawn to read this book at the suggestion of a friend or by your own intuition, believe that only goodness and kindness shall come from this experience and from it, you will know that you are on an eternal journey of God's love and life being lived through you.

> BE OPEN! FEEL! BELIEVE! GROW and KNOW that finding Beauty as you rediscover God in this New Age will be the experience of your lifetime.

Chapter One
In the Beginning ...

W hen I wear my collar and clerical garb out to a New Age gathering, people come up and ask me which religion I belong to. I usually have to hesitate before answering. Those who know me expect a flippant, off-the-cuff remark. But when I am asked *that* question, I go within and my mind reels back to my childhood days in discovery of where I belonged.

I came into this world "in the year of the Lord" 1950. My father was Catholic. My mother was Episcopalian. So what did that make me? I wasn't ever sure. You see, my father had a previous marriage that ended in divorce. He then met my lovely mother. Boldly he went to ask his parish priest what he was to do. **Boldly**, the priest said, **"Get the hell out of my church!"** Hence, I was raised Episcopalian. My father rarely went to church with my mom, sister and me, yet I had no recollection of his being outwardly bitter at his church or God. I later learned that he *was* very hurt and felt that Catholic guilt had been piled on him.

As I grew up in San Diego, California, I faithfully went to Sunday School and must have learned my lessons well. When I was in the fifth grade, I was confirmed in the Episcopalian church and I received my Book of Common Prayer as a gift. I thought this was a good sign of commitment to the church. I can't say I remember my life changed when I was confirmed and had no concept of the Holy Spirit descending upon me, nor did I hear any voice from heaven say, "This is my beloved son in whom I am well pleased." For me personally, I had no feeling that the Episcopalian church, or religion in general, did anything to deepen my awareness of God in my life.

I did have a short stint with the Catholic church when I was in the second grade. Somehow my father happened to bypass a very domineering and strong-willed mother-in-law and got my sister and me enrolled in St. Agnes Catholic Elementary School. Not having been raised Catholic (a meaningful statement I have used often in my life and will use again in this book), I wasn't ready for the rigid and strict nuns that I encountered. My sister's memories include having to go to Mass daily, standing and curtseying when Monsignor or Mother Superior walked in the room and throwing up in front of everyone when it got too hot. I only remember having to take a spelling test and the Sister saying absolutely no questions or no hand raising. Well, I had to go to the bathroom and not being allowed to move or ask to go, I simply ... well, you can guess the rest! Sister wasn't too happy with her new student and I was humiliated in front of the whole class. I remember a few days later my maternal grandmother appeared on the scene and we were put back in public school. So, my short experience with the Catholic church and my longer affiliation with the Episcopalian church left me with no deep understanding of God.

It wasn't until college that I began to think about God in a serious way. Gretchen was a beautiful black woman who worked as the cook in our fraternity. Due to my family dynamics, I turned out to be the shy, quiet child with low self-esteem. When the other guys in the frat house got to me, or situations in my social life or home life were pressing, I always turned to Gretchen for some enlightenment and support. She was a bundle of love and comfort. At that time, her husband, Alva, was dying of emphysema and I would often go over to their house to visit him. He was such a gentle, loving, upbeat man, despite his declining condition. I think in return for my visiting him and for being supportive of his wife during those trying times, he shared with me a loving gift. With almost every subject, whether it be sports, politics, love life ... whatever, he would always talk about Jesus and God, the loving Father. Many times I didn't understand how he could have such a deep relationship with them. How did the day-to-day living with God and Jesus happen in his life? It was all "up there, in my head," as they say. I didn't feel it in my heart, as he did. However, he did plant one of the seeds that would later begin to sprout through its protective cover and hard surface.

It was also during college that I was first introduced to any form of nontraditional or nonChristian religious concepts. We had, at the University of Washington (my family had now moved up to Seattle, Washington and I attended college there), what was known as the Experimental College. This forum offered nontraditional courses that helped one experience life in a new experimental way. A fraternity brother and I signed up for a Transcendental Meditation course, known as TM. TM professed to provide you with a method by which it was possible to achieve real peace in your life. With my family background and struggles in the fraternity I was the first in line to sign up! Finally, I would find a way to make some sense out of the confusion I felt about life and my own identity and direction. Maybe this would lift the fog. Maybe this would make me feel connected to some path of life! I participated in a private ceremony to receive my mantra (a mantra is a word repeated over and over). Then much to my surprise, I began a practice that would help immensely in calming my jitters and shaking hands, and stop the "mind chatter" which engaged me from morning to night. To achieve peace, we were instructed to do this meditation twice a day.

Did this bring me the peace I was looking for? Did it still

this searching mind that was looking for a purpose and a connection with all of life? Of course the answer would be no. I felt let down again with life. The problem, as I saw it, was not that the peace and quiet weren't beneficial and helpful in many aspects of my life, but that this method led me nowhere. It was as though I had reached a dead end. I had come to a door that was impossible to open, but I knew it needed opening. So I quietly released this practice completely and again asked the same question that was a top-ten song back in those days: "What's it all about, Alfie?"

I vividly remember combing the library stacks and the bookstores for books that would help me quench my thirst for answers in my life. One day I came across a book in one of my fraternity brothers' room. The cover of the book had a picture of a young Tibetan boy with a huge bright light coming out of his forehead. The book was entitled *The Third Eye*, by T. Lobsang Rampa. (The term "third eye" refers to an energy center or chakra right in the middle of your forehead, just a bit above the knit of your eye brows. When this energy center is open, one is said to be able to be more clairvoyant, *i.e.*, read people and situations better, trust insights and intuition more.) Within the pages of this book, I became lost in a story of a young man who was on a Spiritual journey of enlightenment. The "elders" of his religion, the monks, helped him experience the truth that there was more to life than just the physical body. He **could** see colors around people and objects. He **could** discern illnesses people had and provide answers and healings for them. He **could** talk to the Spiritual Masters. He **could**, he **could** ... do everything I wanted to do. This was the first time I had seen my dreams, my desires and my envisioned pathway in a concrete form. What was even more exciting was that the cover said the book was based on real, true-life facts! Where could I find out how to open my third eye? Unfortunately, I was let down again. The way Robsang received the opening of his third eye was by the elder Tibetan monks opening a hole in his forehead with a

wooden stake! Not exactly the road to enlightenment I pre-
ferred. So, I shoved that concept under the proverbial bed
and went back to my fogged-up reality.

A Leap of Faith

After college, I was accepted to attend the University of
San Diego School of Law. Since my family had not yet
moved back to San Diego, I lived with a Catholic family.
Something in my brain was stirring and I was thinking
more and more about God, more than likely because of
seeds planted earlier by various people. I made friends with
a young man named Brother Martin, and one day he took
me over to the parish convent for a reason I've forgotten.
While waiting in the foyer for him, I remember reading a
small leaflet called "The Daily Word" which lay on the front
table. It recommended you say "God loves me" with every
step and breath you take each day. Strangely enough, this
exercise stuck in my mind. After several days of repeating
this new mantra, I experienced an eerie sense of peace in my
life. For the first time, I felt loved unconditionally by something greater than a friend or a parent. I understood that it
was God.
Having discover that God loved me so much, I wanted
to join a community that felt this great and deep love for
God. The community at St. Charles Borromeo was so warm
and supportive of someone interested in the Catholic faith.
Brother Martin, who lived at the church, became my best
friend. We lovingly called him Big Al, for not only was he
that, but his heart was also big and full of love. He didn't
have a malicious bone in his "little" big body. Although he
could be very mischievous at times, he was a lover of life
filled with joy and laughter. His was the kind of church I
wanted to be a part of. Martin was one of the first persons
who began asking me to consider the priesthood as a vocation for my life. My heart said "Yes, I want to be a part of
this joy and love of God."

Eventually everything started to fall in place: I became Catholic (still no loud voice from heaven). I worked with the right people who knew what they were talking about regarding marriages and annulments. My Dad's first marriage was annulled ... Mom became Catholic ... AND ... their marriage was blessed (10 points in heaven!). I continued to attribute all this to God. In my heart, I felt this strong push to find a way that I could greater serve this wonderful God. I could show it through my actions as an attorney, but I sensed I was to do it another way. Being around so many "religious" (nuns, brothers and priests), I began to toy with the possibility of entering the seminary. My thinking was based on the hopes that I could eventually become a priest and help others know that they were unconditionally loved by our Creator.

I will never forget the night I was having dinner at home and by mistake (I hadn't yet learned that there are no such things as mistakes), a transcript from college came home instead of going to the seminary. My Dad asked what this was all about and I told my parents that I was thinking of entering the seminary. I heard him tell my Mom as he was walking down the hallway, "Well that's the end of the McNamara line!" Oh well, life happens. And so it did happen: I was accepted into the seminary.

Seminary

I kept my innocence as long as I could throughout my early seminary days. Having just graduated from law school, I only had to spend one year in the minor seminary and didn't have to take some of the college-level theology classes which probably would have bored me out of my mind, or at least made me ask what this had to do with my grander vision. We had a good seminary staff of priests and the politicking was very low profile, at least that I was aware of. I still could go for walks out to the edge of the beautiful campus of the University of San Diego and see the magnificent sunsets. I could drive down to the beach and walk on the edges of the earth or stroll through the green historic parks in San Diego. In all places, I felt one with a wonderful God who loved us all so much and had a plan through us all to make the Kingdom a reality. As I mentioned much earlier in my history, I was not into the "new age" realities yet. I was simply into my present reality, holding fast to my dreams of helping people know they were loved by God, and that they could follow the commandment to love themselves as they loved others.

I remember, however, during my first year of the minor seminary in San Diego, going out to dinner with a casual acquaintance. Sometime during dinner, he started to share with me some strange events that were happening in his life. He had met this former nun named Claire who had given him a book called *God's Way of Life*, by Adele Tinning. He said it was filled with spiritual messages she had received from the "other side" and talked about each individual's purpose here on earth. For some reason, none of that made any sense to me, but I told him I would read it. I later tossed it away when I moved on to the major Seminary. This book became like a bad penny, but in a good sense: it came back again, just when I needed it. The force behind it would be a pivotal point in my life several years down the road.

My first blip on the screen of real life came when the seminary and I decided where I would go for major seminary. I remember a faculty member calling me in and saying he had heard rumors that I was still dealing with issues of my sexual identity and because of that, I shouldn't go on to the major seminary. I should stay back and do some more resolving. A burst of anger went through me and I tried to suppress it in his presence. I calmly told him that it was none of his business and if that were the issue, then it would be discussed solely between my spiritual advisor (my confessor) and me. I raged a little when I got to my advisor. "Who the hell does he think he is delving into gossip about my personal life!"

"Take it easy," said Father Neal.

"Hey," I continued, "I thought this was all about kindness and love and support of one another. And who isn't dealing with identity issues throughout their whole life? Does he have it all together? Do I complain about his idiosyncrasies? Aren't you still dealing with growth issues?"

I was surprised at how upset I was. I felt like someone was trying to burst my bubble. It reminded me of the day I came home from college with four A's and one B+ and my Dad said, "You could have gotten all A's!" (Of course, I questioned him about this years later and he said he only said that in jest.) But that is how I felt in this instance. "Let's focus on the B+," the other priest pried. Hey, I thought God and Jesus looked only at the A's! I didn't know it yet, but what I was beginning to feel was a sense of betrayal. Someone was starting to mess with my dream and I didn't like that! That little turbulence blew over and off I went to the play in the major seminary, with the big boys, so to speak.

Going up to Menlo Park for the major seminary opened a whole new window of what the church was like. We had a pastoral program which allowed us to be assigned to a parish or Catholic high school. Both places would help us know what it would be like to work with the people. My own diocese also had a similar program during the summers when we would return from the major seminary. Both were life savers! Without knowing any of the tenets of the metaphysical ways, I knew that it was in the people that God's presence was felt most. I loved laughing, smiling and having fun with the families or the kids in the parish schools. I had no fear about feeling like that little kid Jesus talked about when he said you must become like a little child to enter into the kingdom of God (Matt. 18:1–4). It was with the Mortons, Gambelins, Elbecks, O'Reilys, Treglias and so many more of the families I came to know during those seminary years that I kept my sanity and felt grounded in God's life on earth. Back at the ranch (I mean the seminary) I began to learn about a different God than the unconditionally loving one I first experienced. The Sulpician fathers were a very educated lot. They taught a God of rules and regulations, cannons, and shoulds and should nots. Fear became a common word in theology and life. So many of the readings in our daily breviary (prayer book) talked of a vengeful God, as mentioned in many of the psalms. God became a technical God and the homilies/sermons preached at our daily liturgies were boring or outdated or over our (my) heads. Once in a while, we would hear from one of the more radical Sulps (Sulpicians) out on their own horizon or one of the diocesan priests assigned to the seminary and less fearful of being more human—one of *us*. Their homilies usually provoked laughter, as well as deep thought. Since we usually had dinner after mass, these priests and their homilies would be the hot topics of discussion as opposed to one of the other "bored-inary" ones.

Fear began to raise its head in our daily life. Little innocent me must have led a sheltered, yet graced, life. I was never aware of fearing others in the real world. I do remember my Dad chiding me to always stand strong and never allow others to walk over me. But that thought just sailed past my mind. Why would someone in life want to walk over another person? Was I from another planet or what? I didn't get it. I thought we all came here to be at peace with one another. No cruelty. No backstabbing. No prejudice. When I was in the junior high youth group in the Episcopalian church, I cried in front of everyone the night we had a black man come speak to our group on prejudice. "We do have the same heart, the same brain, the same body parts, don't we? How can we treat each other differently because of the color of our skin?" I asked.

Now in the seminary, I was beginning to see why others treated people differently. During those years, the seminarians from San Diego were treated quite differently by the

Sulpicians. For some reason, we threatened them. San Diego had a great progressive minor (college) seminary program and jealousy may have played a part in how the Sulpicians treated us. The major seminary at Menlo seemed to be trying to get up with the times. One professor in particular, a priest, used to mock and make wise cracks about the San Diegans in front of all the other "sems" (seminarians). I began to feel as though they were saying, "We are the ones in power. Don't mess with us 'cuz' we can be the ones to bounce you outta here!"

Several of us had a wonderful priest spiritual-advisor who wasn't a "Sulp." He was a favorite among the San Diegans and he would keep us abreast of how to get through the system better. That priest was Father O'Shannesey. We would call him "The O." Because of the politics, gossip and backstabbing in the seminary, I was beginning to feel as though my bubble about God and the church was being ripped open larger and larger. In those frustrating moments, it was great to go for a walk with "The O." He had such a way of laughing and bringing lightness to any situation. He was my band-aid, the one who helped me through disillusion after disillusion. It was the people, he would say, that counted. He encouraged me that, one day soon, I would make it through all this illusion and "they" would be left behind their stone walls, their seminaries. I would be out with the people, happily sharing the love of God. God bless "The O," who has since died. I don't know how he did it. For when I eventually got out to the trenches, many of the same issues were still there. But "The O" had learned how to make it through any storm, shining like a rainbow, ready to shed light wherever he went. I would try to do the same. Quite possibly, it was by or through the graces of my learning more about God via the "New Age" belief systems that my hopes and dreams in a radically loving God stayed alive.

My fellow seminarians helped prevent me from derailing my vision ... some of them, that is. I say some of them because it was amazing to watch how some would fall into the trap of "kissing posteriors" or playing the games like good little boys. But it was my closer friends who would help me relax, smile and laugh behind closed doors or go out to dinner. I remember even going to a race track with them one week night just to get away from it all. Of course, I would bring my books to study while they played! I wasn't as smart as they were! These friends knew when to keep their mouths shut and how to stay centered when the barbs or back-handed comments came. Already feeling some sense of betrayal, I would open my mouth too often to question the system, or ask why my dream world was fading.

My papers and tests always seemed to have a twist to them, never completely agreeing with the party line. I always tried to bring the good out in everything and everyone in a creative way that people could relate to. I wanted to help them feel God more in themselves. Often times, my papers were written in dialog form, as though a historical person were dialoguing with his/her soul or even with God about certain issues of the church. Other papers or presentations were directed from the most extreme outcast's viewpoint: the gay person, the migrant worker, the peasant in South America, the divorced and remarried or the woman's point of view. So, the Fathers weren't too happy with my rebellious ideas, but I passed all my classes, anyway. Thank God we had a great pastoral program that allowed us to go out to individual parishes and be with real people and experience being in the "trenches" with priests who were working with the people on a daily basis. I was fortunate enough to be assigned to one parish priest, Father Joe Bravo, who became a wonderful "real life" mentor to me during those seminary years. He showed the beauty of wonderful, rich, moving, human liturgies, youth retreats and other parish programs involving the people. Most of all, he taught me that it was okay to have the child within me (within us all) come out and play.

One of the major events that refocused my attention on God was the death of my mother. As I write this, it seems so strange that because of the theological content of the material taught in the seminary, my attention was not constantly on God. Although I think I was always challenging and integrating the material on an intellectual level, I rarely felt or contemplated it on a Spiritual level. One would think that reading the breviary (a prayer book containing scripture, prayers and other matter) morning and night, going to Mass every day and attending retreats, that I would have great Spiritual insights and a raising of consciousness. For some reason (since then, I **have learned** there are no accidents or events happening for just "some reason"), my mind was focused on other things. I often was very aware of the repressive tone of a psalm, a homily or an exegesis (an explanation of a biblical passage). That tone hooked me and turned me away from the God within. The time when I felt most at peace was when I was returning to my seat after receiving holy communion. That was a time when all conflict stopped, all mind chatter ceased and peace reigned for a few precious moments.

The death of my Mom released a whole new range of emotions and feelings as to how I related to God. I was angry, very angry and confused that just one year before my ordination to the diaconate, a woman whom I was coming to love and understand on a deep level was gone from my life. I remember several nights after she died. I walked down the street and raised my fist to the heavens and cursed God. Strangely enough, the only response I felt in return was an eerie silence and a sense of peace. For a moment, I was aware of eternity, time unfolding minute by minute. I was able to play the part of the good seminarian and made it through the funeral. I even gave the sermon (homily, as we now call it), telling friends and family that God had chosen to call Mom to heaven as she would be an enhancement of his kingdom above. (I'm not sure I would explain it that way thirteen years later.)

Eight months later, I was ordained a deacon. I could now "hatch 'em, match 'em and dispatch 'em" as we were so fond of saying in the seminary. That is, I could baptize, marry and bury people. This was a wonderful year for me. I experienced what it was really like to live in a worshiping community. Being only a deacon, I was shielded from much of the politics, pettiness and back stabbing that a pastor or associate pastor had to deal with. At my level, the people were gracious, open to a youthful deacon and very supportive of my ideas.

During that year, I went back to the seminary for three two-week workshops. Much to my surprise, during my second workshop, I was placed on probation for nothing more specific than having a "bad attitude." This appeared as one last-ditch attempt by the seminary faculty to deflate my dreams completely. But the Irish pastors of San Diego came to my rescue. "Tanks be to God for the Irish," as they would say in their Irish brogue. Thanks be to God for the Irish clergy, one of whom was my deacon pastor. They pointed out to the seminary board the good work I was doing with the people of God. There were no complaints about my theology or my ATTITUDE. With that type of support, I was off probation and it was onward to priesthood.

God is good and one year after my deacon assignment, on April 22, 1980, I was ordained by Bishop Leo T. Maher, into the priesthood of the Roman Catholic Church for the Diocese of San Diego (or was it for the people of the Diocese of San Diego?). As I look back, I think of Father Don Kulleck's favorite scripture passage from the Gospel of Luke about Jesus and the Road to Emmaus. After the death of Jesus, the town was all a buzz about his death and missing body. Two followers of Jesus were walking on the road, on the way to Emmaus. Jesus joined them but they did not recognize him as he was in a new, unfamiliar, Spiritual body. Finally, they sat down to eat and when Jesus broke the bread and said the blessing, the followers "opened their eyes" and recognized the Christ before them. Beauty and meaning came back into their lives. Jesus then took time to discuss all the events that had happened in his life and all the scripture passages that pointed to this glorious moment in eternal time. This is how I describe what my unfolding years in the priesthood were like. So many times it was, and is, difficult to see Jesus and the Beauty in one form or another, especially when we get stuck in the routineness of rituals. But Beauty does abound. Jesus is in new Spiritual forms each day and we so often fail to recognize him. When we open our eyes and see the all powerfulness of God, God's omnipresence, God's Beauty, we can refer to the wonderful things we have been taught from our traditions in the church as Jesus explained to the two followers on "The Way." We can see how true it is that God is alive and in our world today.

Priesthood

Sometimes it still amazes me to think that I was ordained into a "brotherhood" through a ritual that has been used for almost 2,000 years. Tradition has it, and our beliefs create it, that first Jesus, and then the first bishops and others down the line, have laid hands upon men (and women) as a sign that a priest is dedicated to build the Kingdom of God on earth. When asked how to pray, Jesus said, "Our father who art in heaven, hallowed be thy name. Thy kingdom come, **Thy will be done, on earth, as it is in heaven.**" I need to afford myself the luxury of at least thinking that I have chosen, with God's help, to be an important instrument that can help facilitate the manifestation of the Kingdom of God on earth. Sometimes this is hard to see through that window of ordination. When you are incorporated into a system, you become enmeshed with people who have formed very strong opinions about *their* faith and *their* religion. So headfirst I went, and fortunately, my eyes were opened to a new Spiritual form of Jesus within my first year.

My First Assignment:

Beauty at the Beach
Sacred Heart Parish of Ocean Beach

Nestled in a laid-back, beach community of San Diego, Sacred Heart was filled with a good mixture of people of various ages. Some were retired, others elderly. There were many military, as well as young, enthusiastic families, newly married, and couples whose children had moved out, all were now more active in the church. There were also many high school youths. I was placed in charge of the youth group as one of my main responsibilities. It was through that avenue, as well as in my Sunday homilies, that I began to weave the magic of a loving God in our lives. What a joy it was to bring new light into their lives. I scoured the resources each week in attempts to find new stories, even humorous new jokes, to catch their attention that God was alive and active in their lives. Many responded. Many were secure enough to share new ideas about God, church and community with me.

At my first two assignments, I was very lucky to have Irish pastors. Although not perfect, they were very kind and supportive of me and my innovative ways of talking about my love for God. The senior pastor at Sacred Heart was a gracious, very gentle, faith-filled, supportive Irishman who seemed to revel in the glory of having a young, lively priest in his berg. People commented on how great it was to see the pastor once again laugh and join in all the fun and festivities, to allow innovative ways in sermons, decorations and music to prevail.

My greatest joy was working with the youth. They were even more open to hearing about new avenues to God. Most of them had been in Catholic schools for over eight years and were pretty bored with the routine and rote ways of praying and celebrating God. Their peers were very strong in their magnetic efforts to draw them away from

church and spirituality. But those who came to the high
school youth group were energized and wanted to give back
to the community through service and participation. They
energized me!

In the "adult world," I remember the first time someone
lodged a complaint about me. I had just finished saying
Mass and returned to the sacristy to change out of my vest-
ments. A man who was at mass was waiting for me. He
got pretty close to me and started telling me that I must not
have been trained very well in the seminary.

"What seminary did you go to? What gives you the
right to add words to the sacred liturgy?" he bellowed.

I tried to remain calm and asked him what part of the
Mass he meant. And I politely, but sarcastically, said, "By
the way, what seminary did you spend three years in?"

He said he hadn't gone to the seminary but had been a
Catholic all his life and had never heard a word added to the
Mass before. Well, I told him that I'd had one of the best
liturgists in the United States teach me how to say the Mass.
But, as for the added word, I had learned that from Father
Neal Dolan, my minor seminary spiritual advisor, who had
been a priest for over 25 years. People loved him and he
had never received any criticisms about the way he said
Mass.

"Well," he said, "You haven't heard the last of this." His
and other calls were made to the good-hearted pastor, complaining that I wasn't holding the bread right or that I was
changing other traditional words of prayer into something
more modern. Monsignor Rhatigan would make a "strong
suggestion" to cease or leave out certain practices. "Don't
rock the boat! Let's have a smooth operation. Why cause
problems?" He would say this as though he were advising
his own son in the ways of life. For when he, too, first came
to this parish years before, he had to deal with a lot from
people who harshly and bitterly complained about some of
his new ways. So, although he knew how to stand his
ground, he asked me not to rock the boat!

After the talks or the phone calls, I would go to my room in a state of shock, sadness and dismay. How could people be so blind? Where did they get this tunnel vision? I know I wasn't raised Catholic, but I thought humanity, and especially people in church who preached a Gospel of compassion and peace, would be a bit more gentle. So there began the erosion of my beliefs that all Catholics were kind, loving and supportive people. It is interesting how the perception of priests by the lay people has changed with the advent of Vatican II in the late 1960s. People used to revere priests and put them on a pedestal, never thinking of saying a critical word against them. I would never want to go back to those days where we were placed on high. But, just because we are now eye to eye, that doesn't mean that we are to be disrespectful to each other.

A Door Begins to Open

My first exposure to the unknown happened quite simply and unexpectedly. It was to lead to a whole series of wonderous, strange events. I remember one morning having an appointment with a woman named Mary. Mary was having marital problems and wanted some advice. After we were finished with that subject, she said, "Father, I have something to tell you that you may not understand, but I've got to tell you!" Well, I was still wet behind the ears and trying to meet people where they were coming from, so I told her to go on. She told me that she had recovered from cancer. (I could see that Mary had been through some physical struggles but she looked good and on the up and up.) "Despite the odds," she said, "and the fact that the doctors had told me it was terminal, I'm cured and free from cancer!" I had heard stories about miraculous cures in the past and had tucked them somewhere in the back of my head, hoping to find out more about them when I had time. Time slipped away over the years, but now I was sitting face to face with someone who had professed to experience a real miracle! To officially be declared a miracle, the church has to do an extensive investigation and come to the conclusion that, among other things, no ordinary means could have caused the cure. What I had heard in the past were extraordinary healings **not** documented by the church. These were healings talked about in prayer groups or other faith-filled arenas, not recognized or acknowledged by the church. But now, I was sitting before a miracle in the making!

Wanting to find out more, I asked her, with a big smile on my face (and I must admit, a few butterflies in my stomach), to continue. Mary had heard about a woman named Sister Sarita (not a religious nun) who was a Mexican Curandera, meaning, healer. Sister Sarita had completely healed her of the cancer. "Curandera?" A brief thought swung through the rafters of my mind. "Was she a witch doctor?" "Voodoo?" The overwhelming desire to believe that God could work miracles through ordinary means and ordinary people, brought me back to an even keel. I told Mary I would love to meet the lady. She said, "Great, because Sarita was Catholic and I had told her about this young energetic priest at my parish and she would like to meet you!" So I went down to the barrio, Logan Heights, collar and all, to meet Sarita.

Because Mary told me Sarita was Catholic, I felt much more at ease going into this old, storefront-looking building. However, just down the block was Chicano Park which surrounded a pretty rough part of the neighborhood. So now I was definitely glad I wore my collar! Sarita was a lovely lady. She had a sparkle in her eyes and a warm, friendly smile. Her arms embraced me and she hugged me and looked into my eyes as though I were a long lost friend. Much to my relief, I didn't see any signs of voodoo or witchcraft, only crucifixes, pictures of the Blessed Virgin Mary and Jesus on the walls and (very catholic) lots of candles burning. Spanish was a language in which I was barely fluent. Frustratingly so, that was all Sarita spoke. But I was able to understand that this was a good woman, dedicated to the work of God through the service of healing.

I was very amazed not to be disturbed or frightened by any of the healings that were going on while I was down there. I didn't see or learn about Sarita's own version of psychic surgery until later (I will discuss her techniques in the chapter on that subject). Nevertheless, I was able to see her doing what I presumed were some other forms of healings. She waved her hands around a person as though she were knocking down or off unseen spider webs. (I later found out that she was cleansing a person's aura, their energy field around their body.) Other times she would hold a candle close to their body and move it up and down as if she were illuminating any darkness which had clung to a person. Although I widened my eyes a bit at this unfamiliar practice, I wasn't repulsed or threatened. Many Catholic churches are loaded with candle stands and the analogy of bringing light to the darkness is often used. I was just pleased to see not only Sarita smiling, but also peppering her prayers with words of Jesus, Mary, God, Holy Spirit. I knew the people were in good hands. And, from what I could determine, the people Sarita worked with appeared to feel so much better after their healing session, and said as much. Most of them, also, I was told, were very pleased to see a Catholic priest in their midst!

I set up a time within the next week to say Mass for Sarita and her helpers, as well as any people there for healings. During the liturgy, after communion, she told me that she had the name of a Spiritual guide to give me. I thought, "How could Jesus, in his many Spiritual forms, talk to this woman and tell her the name of *my* guardian angel?" I didn't think this thought out of priesthood elitism. I just hadn't ever been present with a person who was receiving "direct communication" from God ... or whomever. Deep down inside, I was probably very envious! Should more people be able to receive such information to help them down their journey of faith in life? Could I ever be one gifted enough to help people in a such a way? Well, trusting as I was in my priesthood and in my faith that God knows what he is doing, I had her tell me.

"Jorge Primero," she said in Spanish, "an Egyptian doctor and lawyer!"

"Hmmm, muy interesante," I replied. Very interesting indeed, and I then finished with Mass. I was a bit amused over the fact that, as a young boy, I was fascinated with and loved Egypt so much. Then I thought, "Hmmm, a kid who loved Egypt and that kid eventually receiving his law degree. And now he is told he has a guardian angel that is an Egyptian doctor and lawyer!" My ending thought was, "What a trip!" I smiled some more but soon forgot about my new guardian angel, George the First. And he, or I, didn't seem to make any real, deeper connection after that.

I had one more encounter with Sarita while at Sacred Heart. This dealt with a different parishioner, Don, who was very close to death from cancer. Sarita had impressed me so much that I suggested that Don should contact her. Actually, I put on the collar and went with Don and his wife to Sarita's place of work. I was getting pretty brave about doing things and going places that were foreign territory for the church. Sarita said she could not heal the cancer as she did with Mary but could only help Don be at peace. She saw the beautiful Angel of Death and knew that it was his time to pass over. Strangely enough, this information brought great peace of mind to Don and his wife. It also placed quite a different light on the dying, death and grieving processes of this Catholic couple. It wasn't what they had expected from a priest. First a suggestion that they consult a healer. Then, after discovering that not much could be done, they should face death in a very positive way with no fear of condemnation or judgment. They said that they had received so much love from Sarita and from their parish priest. They trusted that we were representing the loving, caring, compassionate God whom Don was soon to meet. And this loving, beautiful Angel of Death that Sarita described, watching over and guiding Don, certainly did not cause any fear in them or me. I felt no shame in having brought them a wider understanding of who God is, despite the fact that they had never heard of such a process of death and dying in their traditional Catholic teachings. Again, the fruits of the message were there: peace, love and a sense of holy communion with God. I was proud I could help them share in this truth.

God bless my pastor, Monsignor John Rhatigan. As mentioned, he was a beautiful, good-hearted, well seasoned, Irish pastor. I was a young priest trying to stimulate the parishioners with enthusiasm and light in the most unique ways. If he had known I was taking some of "his parishioners" (pastors are supposed to be very territorial at times) down to a Spiritual healer, I'm not sure he would have ... on second thought, he did seem to love me a lot and love breaks down a lot of false, blocking barriers. If he did find out, I am sure that all he would have asked for was no "public scandal." However, I never got to test that out as I was transferred to the local Catholic high school at the beginning of my third year of priesthood.

For some reason (Ha! Remember, for a fact now: accidents never happen), I elected to teach a senior course on *Death and Dying* at the high school. Maybe I subconsciously wanted to work out some of my feelings about my Mom's death. Maybe it was a push from God to try to open my doors about death and life. We had no extensive class or workshop on death and dying in the seminary. We had learned that death was a very sacred moment. As a priest, we would have to be there during the stages of dying, if the person dying was conscious, and equally important, for the family of those dying. Compassion, they taught in the Pastoral Theology course, was the operative word in dealing with both. But the theology of death was not greatly explored. The belief system of the church could be stated in simple and basic terms: lead a good life, go to confession often, receive the sacraments and when you died, you would be welcomed into heaven ... or at least the initial stages of heaven (least we forget about purgatory!). If you were really bad and didn't do all the above, you risked the chance of going to hell, forever being separated from God. At this stage in my life, I didn't feel it was all that black and white, yet I had no in-depth understanding of the complete truthful process. In other words, I was very comfortable with the fact that I was able to still search and seek deeper meanings about death and dying.

I was amazed at how much more the teacher's manual at the high school taught about the stages and phases of death and dying. We, teacher and students, did learn much from a section on the stages of death, based on the life teachings of Elisabeth Kübler-Ross, the foremost expert on death and dying. (The stages are, not necessarily in order, denial, anger, bargaining, depression and acceptance.) All these new understandings made death so much more "earthy," human, and less mysterious. I wanted to learn more! I vividly remember one day, back at the parish after school, walking by a magazine table and seeing the face of Elisabeth Kübler-Ross on the cover of *People Magazine.* I read in the article that she lived just outside San Diego in Escondido. I have no idea how I got her phone number, but I called her up and told her who I was, what I was teaching and asked if I could have a meeting with her. Well, as luck would have it (!), she was coming into town for a doctor's appointment and I could meet her at the International House of Pancakes for coffee. Close encounters with God are in the *most* unusual places! We met and had a wonderful talk. I remembered looking into her deeply Spiritual eyes, wondering what adventures she would lead me on to new horizons. What ways would she show me to find Beauty in life as she has? She encouraged me to go to one of her "Life, Death and Transition" workshops so I could learn more about her work and maybe even learn more about those issues in my own life.

The workshop was fantastic and she was right: I did learn more about me! I realized how difficult it was to get in touch with my feelings. I had a great deal of difficulty at that time participating in an exercise to release "stuck stuff" from the past. I still remember Elisabeth prodding me on, not to be embarrassed, to let go of my weaknesses, share, share, feel safe! I did sense that there must have been a lot of fear about tapping into the pain of past experiences of mistakes or growth which may have created pockets of anger or self-doubt. Imagine that! A priest, one who is an instrument of reconciliation and communion with God, having trouble being reconciled within himself. I can only guess how difficult it must be for lay people to get through these moments in their own lives. Maybe that was one of the reasons the lines to the confessional were/are so short. Fear! This only made me more determined to continue to find effective ways to bring peace into people's lives.

I did bring back to my ministry a very valuable exercise which Elisabeth conducted at the end of the workshop. Many of the people on the weekend were dealing with terminal illnesses. She provided each of us with a pinecone and then asked us to stand up before the crowd, in front of a fireplace. We were to write on a small piece of paper a few words which represented baggage we needed to let go of, especially important for those ready to soon make the transition in death. We then, voluntarily stood up, and shared with the crowd this information. This was the most moving and cathartic experience I have ever seen. Grown men and women letting go of years of shackles and chains which they had been carrying about themselves, their family or spouses/partners. Tears, laughter, sobs and soul-felt feelings were expressed and released in one final symbolic gesture. The pinecone and note were released into the fire. They snapped, crackled and burnt into the oblivion of forgiveness and forgetfulness. I have since used this exercise on many retreats with high school students, especially seniors ready to move on to new horizons. It is amazing how much junk they had collected about themselves in such a short time span. I had each round of statements end with rousing, accepting applause from their fellow classmates. Most experienced true feelings of reconciliation and a realignment with who they truly are: loved individuals. Elisabeth ended the workshop with a short statement that this is what it will be like when we get to heaven: unconditional love from God. In my efforts with the students, as well as the people in the parish, I tried my hardest to integrate this message of total unconditional love from God (no guilt or fear about death or life) into their theological understanding of God, life and death.

What turned out to be the most serendipitous event during the workshop was when Elisabeth told us that we were all here on earth for a specific reason and had a specific lesson to learn. (That definitely had no place in Catholic teachings ... except for the general fact or lesson that we are here to learn to love God, self and others.) She then proceeded to read each lesson and purpose out of a little white book with green print called *God's Way of Life*! That was the very same book that was given to me by my dinner companion years before when I was in the seminary. It was the one I had trashed. Now I was becoming totally fascinated by the connections of all the metaphysical events that were being brought before me. (By the way, my lesson was "Patience." Bingo!) Out of my desire to learn as much as I could about God and our purpose in life, I asked Elisabeth if she knew where this woman, Adele Tinning, lived. As luck would have it (again!), she told me she lived in San Diego. Elisabeth was sure that if I went to one of Adele's monthly meetings and told her I was a Catholic priest and that I knew her (Elisabeth was a good friend of Adele's and had visited her often) that Adele would talk to me. Little did I know how that predicted outcome would catapult me into a world of great adventure, and a world filled with visible signs of God's presence.

Adele Tinning:
Beauty in a 70-year-old Sweetheart!

Settling back in San Diego, I found out that Adele was at the Swedenborgian Church on Friday night. I was a little nervous about going ... too chicken to go by myself for several reasons. Again, I knew she would be "talking" with spirit and, although I was excited about learning how to find out more about God, this was still a totally foreign area for Catholics. And despite how outgoing I may appear to be at times, I have a real shy side and feel much more comfortable in numbers (friendly numbers!). Okay, maybe I was afraid someone would say, "What the hell are you doing at an event like this, Father? I'm gonna tell the Bishop on you!" So I took with me Margaret Alvarez, a wonderful, understanding and supportive friend and parishioner from Sacred Heart. I felt comfortable with her next to me as she had been such a strong "buttress" for me in my novice first year or two as a young priest. She (and her family) gave me strength to "go for it" in shaky and/or innovative situations.

After saying a prayer to Jesus to make sure I was on the right path and that somehow this would further help me to know his presence in our world, we headed out for the meeting. We went early and asked at the front door if they knew where Adele Tinning was. They directed my attention to this wonderful, white haired, grandmotherly woman. She turned around, smiled and beamed with God's presence. So here I stood in my priest collar in front of this beautiful woman and I said, "I'm a Catholic Priest and I know Elisabeth Kübler-Ross." Well, you would think I had just told her I was Jesus in a priest collar (not to be sacrilegious!).

She said, "Oh honey, it's so good to have you here and that Elisabeth is such a wonderful lady. When it comes time to ask someone to sit at the table, you just come right up first." "The table?" What was she talking about "sitting at the table"? As she talked to the group for about an hour-

and-a-half, she explained to us what it meant to "sit at the table." She talked about her gift of communicating with "Spirit" through the means of their energy coming into the table. She said the Spirit and its energy actually lifted the table off the floor at an angle and tapped the table on the floor and went through the alphabet, stopping at the desired letter, to give a message. Adele was at least 70 years old and her hands were very arthritic. With her hands on top of the table, she absolutely couldn't be moving this table by herself. Impossible! (See the following picture of me at the table with Adele for the first time, after I took off my collar.)

She said that not only were you given a message when you "sat at the table," Jesus also spelled out who your Master Teacher was. "Lord Jesus," I silently prayed, "Help me know what I'm getting into! You're supposed to come into the table and tap out a name of a Master Teacher?" It sounded like Sister Sarita, telling me about Jorge Primero. I must admit I felt there were a lot of butterflies doing a conga-line dance in my stomach. I knew this nervous feeling didn't come from fear that I might be doing something evil, or the devil would get me. If anyone looked into Adele's eyes or heard her message, they would feel secure and safe. As I will mention in the chapter about channeling, to see whether something is "good or bad." If you want to play that game—you do as Jesus said to do: you look at the fruits of the "tree"/message. Adele spoke of love, kindness, charity, hope, and yes, most often about God and Jesus. My fear of anything evil happening to me couldn't have logically been the reason for my dancing friends down below.

Well sure enough, when it came time for the demonstration, Adele called me up. A wonderful sense of peace and serenity came over me as I sat at the table and we began communicating with Spirit. The table started to tilt up on two legs very gently. It really did feel like a gentle, holy spirit reverently lifted up one end of the table. I checked out Adele's hands, wrists and arms and there didn't appear to

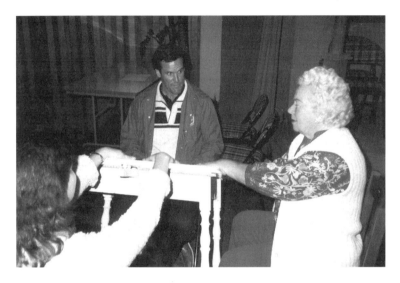

Author with Adele Tinning

be any pressured being applied from them. She continued
to have that angelic smile and twinkle in her eye. She
almost looked like Mrs. Santa Claus after baking her hubby
his favorite cookies. You can't imagine how calming this
was for me. No thoughts of evil ever crossed my mind. I
just sat back and enjoyed the peaceful energy . I did think,
"This must have been what the disciples and friends of
Jesus felt when he was around.

Tapping down on the floor for each letter, Spirit told me
that my Master Teacher was John, the Beloved Disciple.
This information also helped me feel at ease. A Christian,
Catholic saint! I was in "good hands," as the commercial
says. I could also easily accept this as I had *somehow* been
drawn to him during the seminary. Maybe this was
because I thought John was a young man also in search of
the divine. And when John found the divine (Jesus), the
divine told him that the Kingdom of God (the divine) was
inside of him.

Back at the table, when it came time to talk to someone
who had passed over to the other side, I said I wanted to
talk to my mother. Adele asked that I concentrate on my
mother and ask my mom to tap out her name. Adele didn't
know me or my mom from Adam and I was quite (pleas-
antly) surprised when the table tapped out E – L – I – Z – A
– B – E – T – H. The table moved closer to me and then tilted
over on one leg and brushed a side of the table up against
my chest. A wave of energy went through me and I was
momentarily blown away! Then here is where my skep-
ticism came up. I thought now was the time to show the
proof of the pudding. I knew my Mom pretty well and
could now easily test the validity of the answers. We had
a pleasant "yes" and "no" conversation. Still, I wasn't completely sure it was my Mom, but that earlier energy sure felt
like an unconditional loving hug from her! However, I did
feel as though I got a confusing, mixed-message from her
when I asked her if she liked my work at the high school.
She tapped out "yes." Then I asked her if I would be there

next year? She tapped "no!" with a strong bang on the floor. "No?" I thought, "Well, as in real life, maybe she was just a bit confused because I **was** planning to be there for a long time."

Hmmm! Within the next year, I got notice that I was being moved out of the high school and into a new parish. God does move in mysterious ways! When this happened, it made me think back to the moment at the table with Adele and added quite a bit of credibility to this form of communication with Spirit. This move from the high school also facilitated more opportunities to discover Jesus in the multidisguised ways of His and God's presence in this world.

I want to share with you Adele's final comments at the end of my turn with Spirit at the table. Adele said that some one named Claire O'Classen was there in the audience. "Stand up, Claire," Adele commanded. "This is a wonderful woman who plays the piano very well ... AND she is an ex-nun!," she said. That should have been my first clue as to how *my* priesthood would be announced in the future by Adele and how people would come to me and ask, "What are you doing here, Father?"

With the transfer out of the high school and a few problems in my personal relationships, I went through some pretty rough times. One day, for some comfort, I thought I would give Adele a call. Her husband, Oger, answered in a very firm voice. "She's too busy to talk to anyone. She is tired and needs a rest." Oger, I learned later, was just being protective of his wife who said that over 5,000 people had been to her house to learn of their Master Teachers and talk to their loved ones who passed over to the other side. So, I decided to call Claire O'Classen and had a great meeting with her. Claire is very psychic and intuitive and has helped counsel many people along their journey in life. We talked of our new unfolding understanding of spirit as well as sharing old stories about my seminary and priesthood days and her days in the convent. She must have been such a "bright light" when she was in the convent. I remember her telling me one story about how the older nuns would bring her a shoe box of burnt out light bulbs. Claire had a special talent/gift of holding them (the old bulbs!) in her hands and "waa-laa" they would work again. She was a "bright light" indeed in so many ways! One day, she asked me if I wanted to go over to see Adele. You can imagine me jumping into the car probably before I got a "yes" out! We got to Adele's and entered the house of sweetness.

Adele was a lover of God and a lover of candy. She had more candy dishes around the house than was in a See's Candy store. Never was her refrigerator without a piece of pie. Never did we go out to lunch or dinner except to establishments that had the best desserts. She always came home with another pie or cake! That sweet tooth of hers was merely a small reflection of her ravenous appetite to share God with people. Over the years, I saw come through her home, hundreds of sick people, healthy people, happy people, sad people, rich people, poor people, common people and celebrities such as Shirley MacLaine, Elisabeth Kübler-Ross, Patti Page, Robert Shields and Lorraine Yarnell (mimes Shields & Yarnell), Rick Hurst (Cleatus from Duke of Hazzard fame), Dennis Weaver, Barbara Walters, singer Stevie Nicks and many more. They would pass through this house of sweetness and leave with a smile on their faces, contentment in their hearts and probably a few more pounds on their hips.

Among the many Spiritual gifts that Adele had was her ability to be a conduit for God and the Spirit-guide world. This is very different from channeling, which will be explained in a subsequent chapter. Adele was able to sit down at a table (any shape or size, as long as it wasn't fastened down) and call upon the energy of Jesus to mobilize the table, so to speak, to move and communicate by tapping out the alphabet. This is a slow, long and arduous method, one letter at a time. Many claimed an added benefit from sitting at the table was the ability to feel the energy of the Master in the table at that time. (Often times people even received physical healings from and through the energy of Jesus and/or their Master Teacher.) The vast majority of Masters who came to meet us through the table were Christian-oriented. Jesus was usually first in the table. His energy and movement was gentle, loving and reverential. No fast, jerky, strong movements as would come from many of the Old Testament Masters. After Jesus was through telling you about your lesson in life, he would become the gateway for your Master Teacher to come through. It would usually be an apostle or one of the women of the Old Testament. As I think back at the many times I observed people receiving their Master Teacher, I recall hearing names such as Jesus, Paul, Peter, John the Baptist, David, John the Beloved Disciple, Mary, Ruth, Luke, Esther, Matthew, Mark, Thomas and many more. Of course, I thought this means of communicating with, let's say Jesus, was quite different from our Catholic tradition. For most Catholic and other Christians, prayer consists of petitions ... one-sided conversations. Rarely did I hear anyone tell me as a priest that they had "received" a communication from Jesus, God or any spirit. (More on that subject in the next chapter.) However, when I listened to the messages that were coming through Adele and this means of communication, they were all full of love, Beauty, forgiveness and acceptance. And they all reflect back the Beauty within and around ourselves, affirming the goodness of who we are. So, I had no knee jerk reaction to reject these experiences and again, I found myself in the situation of the disciples on the road to Emmaus: open to Jesus, open to new beauties and the Truth in new forms.

One person I met at Adele's would become an influence during an important growth period later in my life. She is a woman who had, and still has, a wonderful magic about her. She always took the new information she received from Adele and all her many table visitors to heart. She filtered, integrated, processed, grew and explored like a pioneer searching out new horizons. She progressed on her own road toward enlightenment. She became a new model, an inspiration for me, of the real-life potential and possibility for growth. Her name is Jacque Snyder. Many times Jacque was at Adele's house when I whirled in, collar and all.

On the first Friday of every month, Adele would rent a large meeting room at the Scottish Rite Temple in Mission Valley. It would be standing-room only, with at least 300 people in attendance. Adele would give a talk for about one hour. After a break, she would give a demonstration, much like the meeting that I attended at the Swedenborgian Church months before. Before the break, she would open the room up to questions and answers. Having heard the talk many times at various meetings and at her home, I would usually stand in the back of the room so that I could slip in and out to chit-chat with friends, new and old. Inevitably, during the questions and answers, Adele would say, "Now I'm probably not supposed to say that he's a priest, so we won't have Father Pat, who is standing in the back of the room, come up and say anything. But you know, my cousin was also a Catholic priest and this young man (she was always most flattering!) is doing so much good with the young people by telling them how much God loves them!"

Often times when I first went to the meetings, I would catch myself scrunching down the wall in the back, thinking, "Oh my God! What if the bishop finds out!" Eventually, I stood tall and found it just another opportunity to talk to people about the goodness of God in our world and in our hearts.

That is where the question, "How do you do it, Father?" got started. People began coming up to me during the break or would later see me at Adele's house and ask me how I integrated all "this New Age stuff" with Catholicism and priesthood. The same circumstances happened and the same questions were asked at each new step along the road in my search for new Beauty and enlightenment within and beyond the four walls of the church. **"How *do you* do it,**

Father?" "How do you find God and Beauty in these new horizons?"

So, let me tell you the background of **"why"** I do it. That will help you understand **"how"** I do it and ... how and why you can too!

Chapter Two
Channeling
"Speak, Lord, I'm Listening"

Channel? What's a channel? Well, there's a channel on the TV! There's a river channel, which directs the flow of a body of water. There is also the religious channel, which we hear about in the Prayer of St. Francis: "Lord, make me a channel of your peace." But Lord, how or what is a channel? The one on TV is a set spot where a signal comes through. The river channel is a structure through which a force of water flows; it can be laid out to direct the water where **"we"** want the water to go ... or is it where **"you"** want it to go, Lord? But what about that channel in the religious sense? How did Francis mean that we, you and I, become a channel of the Lord's peace? Sure I could love more. I could be better to myself more often. Surely, I could be better to others. We could talk about God more and not be so afraid of what others think. But I, personally, know that I never seem to be satisfied about how I am a channel of peace for the Lord. Help! God! I need some instruction!

Well, I could go to the documents of the church to see how I am supposed to be a channel, to live a peaceful life. But there are no church documents on such a subject. Or I could find a guru (did you know that g.u.r.u. stands for Gee! You Are You!?!) and the guru would tell me how to live. Or maybe I could think about the TV analogy, realizing that I could tap into that signal that comes to the "peace channel" and voice that channel, put it on the screen, so to speak. Or I could just go right to God, to the Lord, and ask him how to be a channel of peace! After all, sacred scripture does talk about God giving instruction in several places:

> Moses, however, said to the Lord, "If you please, Lord, I have never been eloquent, neither in the past, nor recently, nor now that you have spoken to your servant; but I am slow of speech and tongue." The Lord said to him, "Who gives one man speech and makes another deaf and dumb? Or who gives sight to one and makes another blind? Is it not I, the Lord? Go, then! It is I who will assist you in speaking and will teach you what you are to say." Yet he insisted, "If you please, Lord, send someone else!" Then the Lord became angry with Moses and said, "Have you not your brother, Aaron the Levite? I know that he is an eloquent speaker. ... You are to speak to him and put the words in his mouth. I will assist both you and him in speaking and will teach the two of you what you are to do. He shall speak to the people for you: he will be your spokesman, and you shall be as God to him." (Ex. 4:10-16)

and,

> "Speak Lord, I am listening. Plant **your** word down deep in me. Speak Lord, I'm **listening**; please show me the way." (1 Sam. 3:9,10) (Emphasis mine.)

As I write this chapter, I realize I have gained so very much more confidence in my ability to listen to God speak to me. We, as Catholics or Christians, are not typically trained to listen for a message from God. But I especially feel this when it comes time to write my homilies for Sunday. Sometimes I am amazed where the "stuff" comes from that I put down on paper. BUT, it has taken a long time to get here.

Before I was "here," I felt I had to rely completely on other people's ability to be clear channels of this *Source* from which I was seeking information. I presumed others had a clearer station tuned in, so to speak, or that they had built their banks of the river channel in a much better way to direct the flow of the master's voices, to receive information from the other side. (Let it be defined here that a channel is one who receives either verbal or intuitive information from the other side.)

Before we get into who these voices are, I think it is important to consider where they come from. I feel they come from the other side. The "other side" ... what do I mean by that? It's interesting how we call it the other side. The other side of what? What I mean is the other side of the physical world. That still sounds odd. I have often asked in the confessional, when someone says they feel far away from God, "Where does God start and we stop?" (The answer is: there really is no line of demarcation.) But for the purposes of this chapter, the "other side" is a term used for the place where people go who have made the transition from what is traditionally called life into death. Being the enlightened souls that you all are, you know that death is not really the end of things, but just a transition, a marker along the journey of eternity. I have come to tell people now that death is just like going to sleep. Then, as if you were waking up in the morning, you get out of bed ... but this morning when you look back to your bed, you see your physical body still lying there. You then float up to and through the ceiling and eventually back to the *Source* for a review of your life and then on (to another chapter!) from there. This dimension, in which you no longer have a denseness, mass or matter to your existence, is one way of describing the "other side."

Who are these from the "other side?" Many believe that there are Masters or Master Teachers, on the other side who are desirous of helping us on this side to grow, learn and proceed onward. Catholics, in particular, would call these Jesus, Mary, saints, your guardian angels, or the Holy Spirit. The Catholic church places some pretty rigid parameters on who these Spirits are and how they can talk to you. A saint must be pre-defined by the church and meet certain requirements. They have to be dead for some time, lead a worthy life and performed two miracles (sometimes more) through intercessory prayer after he or she has died. The official definition of guardian angels is still undefined. But if it works, if they work, go for it! I believe that if you open your consciousness a bit more, you can benefit greatly from their wisdom and guidance. You will see Beauty in the message and these messengers.

Speaking of messengers, that is exactly how the church defines angels—that is, "messengers of God." The Old Testament is jammed packed with stories of angels. Just to mention a few, they appear to Jacob in a vision, descending and ascending on ladders (Gen. 28:12); to Lot as they convinced him to move out of Sodom (Gen. 19); to Daniel by Gabriel (Dan. 8:16); and as foretellers of Samson's birth (Judges 8). In the older biblical translations, Zechariah appears to be having an inner dialog with an angel (Zech. 1:9). This is closer to my definition of channeling than a later biblical version which says an angel came to be with him. In all cases, they appear to be instruments through which God communicates to people on earth. They are an indication of God's deep desire to engage, to communicate with humanity.

In the New Testament, the most obvious occurrences are at the announcements of the births of John the Baptist and Jesus, and angels appearing to Jesus in the Garden of Gethsemane. Jesus even tells us, "When people rise from the dead, they neither marry nor are given in marriage but live like angels in heaven (Matt. 22:30).

There is another reference which seems to imply that we all have our own, personal guardian angels. Matthew 18, verses 10 through 11 say, "See that you never despise one of these little ones. I assure you, *their* angels in heaven constantly behold my heavenly Father's face." In a commentary about angel's appearance in the bible, Saint Jerome says, "*The dignity of a soul is so great, that each has a guardian angel from its birth.*" (I believe some have several.)

Finally, we know that there are many other levels of heavenly communities when Saint Paul tells us that Christ was raised "high above every principality, power, virtue and dominion" (Ephes. 1:21). Saint Gregory the Great presents a clear picture of the church's belief: "We know on the authority of Scripture that there are nine orders of angels, *viz.*, Angels, Archangels, Virtues, Powers, Principalities, Dominions, Thrones, Cherubims and Seraphim."

You will find and come to trust that there are many other teachers who number far greater than those set by the church. And you will find a greater wealth of information, comfort and strength when you "tap into" all of these spirits, accredited or nonaccredited by the church. I think we must be open to all of them as a part of the *Creator Source*, that source, that river of All That Is. It is all from the same source that the saints and angels come from, the same God ... for "All That Is," is God.

In order for one to be certain that they are receiving clear communication (and not that of a Spirit who is still in a greater process of understanding and growth, and has not yet reached the Master Teacher stage), it is important that a certain process or procedure be followed. This is not to say that only one technique or process has to be followed. What I am saying here is that it is important that the channel (you or me) who wants to be open to this higher source, have that intent for clear, higher communication and be clean themselves, so as not to muck up, distort or filter the message being received. Two things must be done. First, follow some type of procedure, one you feel comfortable with and that covers all the bases. Start off with a prayer stating your intent to be a clear channel for God. Then, give permission for one of the Masters, and only a Master, to speak through you. Ask that this communication be clear, concise and concrete. Know that this information shall not only be for your highest good, but also for that of all humanity, for when you are in communion with Spirit, just like the ripple effect upon a pond, the whole world is affected. Then bless your body and all its energy centers (chakras—there are seven), especially your throat and third-eye centers for clear communication. Touch these centers with your hands and visualize God's light, God's love, God's "hands" being there. The second part of the process is to step aside, stating that intent to do so, and allow God to speak to you. This, then, gets into who, or how God, is speaking through a channel. Which doorway, which river, through which aspect of God is God speaking?

We, of course, can communicate or receive messages from God through nature. But this is about the voice form of channeling. I have had the privilege, honor, and pleasure of speaking with God through many channels of communication, **by voice**, that is. It is amazing how new avenues of God come my way. My first news of God communicating through another's body and voice was that of Ramtha. Ramtha is a Master Teacher who walked the earth in ancient times 35,000 years ago. He speaks through a woman named JZ Knight. The phenomena of watching and listening to a video of Ramtha speak through a woman was, and still is, mind-boggling ... it tweaked my own mind to be open to another new experience with God. (Go to your local metaphysical bookstore and rent a video of Ramtha or Lazaris. It will "tweak" your mind, too. And remember to be discerning ... take only what will be for your highest good and grandest vision of who you are.

After hearing about Ramtha, my next close encounter, really my first live encounter with God through a channel, came through Ecton, a Spirit who spoke through Richard Lavin. Richard was a young man living in San Diego. Although I have no present recollection of how I met Ecton, I do remember I was awestruck by this encounter. Have you ever seen the movie *Jonathan Livingston Seagull*? If you haven't, go out and rent it right now! It's about you and me. There are scenes in the movie in which Jonathan, the "bird," sees a horse nursing its young. In another scene, Jonathan encounters an otter and a whale. It's the first time he has seen any of these other creations of God, other forms of Beauty beyond his flock. That's how I felt when I spoke with Ecton! What a wonderful, utterly new form of communication with God. I remember the main message I received from Ecton was, "I would be a multilevel communicator." This message stuck with me, and has encouraged me not only to seek new avenues to find God, but also to find new ways to share God's message with others and to have the conviction to do so. I had also received a message about another lifetime, but I will save that for later. This was my first real encounter with another person channelling. My next first-hand encounter would be one that carried a most important message. The messenger was White Eagle, the one who would teach me that I, too, could flow with and in the river of God—as a channel.

One Spring, I attended a workshop-type retreat in Missouri, given by Ken Carey. I went with my good, "spirit-journeying" buddies, Claire O'Classen, Rick and Shelley Hurst and Elisabeth Kübler-Ross. In Ken Carey, I experienced Beauty, embodied Spirit and soul, in another man. Ken Carey is the author of *Starseed Transmission*, an excellent book about our world's future. He told us that he channelled this book from a higher source. This channelling was induced by the beautiful setting within a green forest with a flowing river running through it. (It was in this same peaceful setting that I was able to share in the celebration of the recommitment of his wedding vows with his lovely wife, Sherry.) This setting opened him up to higher levels of communication yielding the aforementioned book and several other excellent books that have followed. While I was attending this retreat, I met a wonderful woman named Jill who channelled White Eagle, a native American Indian. She seemed to be able to do this on the spot, without saying a verbal prayer or going through any type of a ritual. As I remember, we were waiting for a session out at a picnic table and she said that White Eagle had something to say to us all. After she closed her eyes for a few moments, she opened them again and looked "funny." She then began to speak like an Indian. I really don't remember what the messages were. I was just so awestruck to see and hear again a Spirit speaking through a human being! But then later someone reminded me that White Eagle told me that he could speak just as easily through me as he did through Jill. All I remember saying was, "Well, thank you."

"Well, thank you!" What a strange response to a gift of a Spirit speaking through me! If ever, ... no, *whenever* you awaken to the gift of Spirit speaking through you, please ... please, be a bit more excited! Expressing my feelings about God in my life has become a bit easier since that time.

ANYWAY ... finally, during my flight home, when I relaxed in my seat and closed my eyes, I heard this same Indian voice in my head. It said that White Eagle was very delighted to talk with me and among other things, told me again how much God loves me. I was sitting next to Claire at that time and he told me he also had some personal advice regarding her work with Spirit. He wanted to speak through me. I opened my eyes immediately ... very wide! I told Claire and she encouraged me to "go for it." So I closed my eyes and allowed White Eagle to speak through me, using my voice. The phenomenon was definitely something new for me. There was no lag time, no mental mind analysis. I seemed to have no conscious thought at all about the process while the channeling was going on. It seemed so natural. Yet, it was not as grand as I had envisioned it would be, as dramatic as when he spoke through Jill, or Ramtha spoke through JZ. But I seem to forget at times that even God, working within us, usually begins with baby steps.

As the months unfolded, I remember channelling White Eagle to some of my very close friends. These friends, Rob, Chris, Rod, Irv and a few more courageous souls, were young adults open to new horizons and avenues of theology. Most of them had been raised Catholic—baptized, received First Holy Communion, confirmed. But they were still searching for a deeper spiritual meaning in life, connected with God. I think, in many ways, they looked to me, a (semi-) young, rebellious priest, to be a model for how they could one day expand beyond the traditional four walls of the church.

However, for some reason, I did not allow the new experience of channeling White Eagle to really sink in. It did, however, open me up to the fact that Spirit is able to speak **through me**. Although the messages were not earth-shattering or prophetic (I have since learned that they don't have to be), they seemed to be ones that helped in the managing of my everyday life experiences. Looking back, I think I really didn't take as great advantage of this relationship with White Eagle as I could have, but I'm sure it did ground me more than I could have ever known, as well as open doors to new adventures.

During these initial periods of channelling, I also allowed a few other teachers to speak through me. You may ask, "Was I ever afraid of an evil possession?" The answer for various reasons, is "no." Yes, biblically speaking, there are "bad" angels/spirits (1 Cor. 15:24; Ephes. 2:2; Matt. 25:41; 2 Peter 2:4). But sacred scripture also mentions discernment of spirits. Jesus talks about how you will know a true prophet. You will know them by their deeds, their "good fruit" (Matt. 7:15-23). St. Paul, in his letter to the Galatians, reminds us to live in freedom, guiding our lives by the spirit. Sure signs of not living by the law of the spirit are hostilities, bickering, jealousy, outbursts of rage, selfish rivalries, dissensions, factions, envy and the like. But the "fruits of the spirit," the law of the spirit, is "love, joy, peace, patient endurance, kindness, generosity, faith, mildness and chastity" (Gal. 5:13-26).

In the *Encyclopedia of Theology, the Concise Sacramentum Mundi*, world-renowned, Catholic theologian, Karl Rahner says,

> "Attempts by students of comparative religion to reduce states and experiences such as prophetic inspiration and mystical ecstasy

(where these are genuine) to a common denominator with possession, ignore an essential difference between the two sorts of
phenomena. Possession has a destructive effect on the human
person, while mystical and prophetic experiences work on the spiritual center of the free person, even when they are experiences as
the inescapable grip of the divine."

He later goes on to say in an even stronger way to allay the
fears of "evil possession,"

"Angelology makes it clear that the evil 'principalities and powers'
are a condition of the supra-human and relatively universal character of evil in the world and must not be trivialized into abstract
ideas, but at the same time that these supra-humans and relatively
personal principles of wickedness must not be exaggerated ... into
powers opposed to the good God who are almost his equals in
might. They are not God's rivals, but his creatures."

As one final safeguard, you can also test a spirit by
asking it if it believes in Jesus Christ came in the flesh.
(1 John 4:2). I never strictly used this criteria but my
guarded intent was to allow only Spirits of the highest
integrity and honor to speak through me. I trusted my discernment powers and my belief that God is more powerful
than anything in getting through to me. Although I didn't
use a set "procedure," as I do now when I formally channel,
I know that I at least set the boundaries for the "good guys"
to come on in (as opposed to those still at lower stages,
lower "principalities," of learning).

Most interesting was a handicapped, Tibetan monk,
named Lapsa, who came through and offered insight on
prayer and meditation. He didn't say much, but through
him being in communion in my body, I could experience the
actual peace he experienced through years of training in
mediation. When he was present, I felt at one with the
world and at peace with myself. The focus or lessons were
predominantly centered on the world and me, and not much
was directed toward communication or communion with the
Source, per se.

From the time of White Eagle to this writing, I have sat

before and listened to many a Master Teacher. Adele, through the means of table-tipping, brought forth one of my Master Teachers, John the Beloved Disciple. His message, "Simply trust that God is working with you in your growth," was one that was very frustrating to me back then.

Diana Hoerig, another woman who has found the true meaning of Beauty/God in life, is an amazing channelling friend of mine who channels, among other Spirits, Merlin the magician. Merlin has such magical messages of joy and humor to lighten our journey along the way. Diana did a channelling session for me in which she channelled Lord Orion, a Spiritual, space being (as in outer), of the lineage of Merlin. I will never forget his message. He lovingly told me that now was the time to take up my "shield and sword" and fight as a peaceful warrior for the coming of the Kingdom on Earth as it is in Heaven . No longer was I to experience other people's pain, as I had done previously in order to learn compassion, empathy and sympathy. "Stand up **NOW** and fight for the truth!" Orion commanded. That session hit me like a brick and I cried and cried and cried some more as the words of wisdom were shared with me. My natural tendency is not to feel the deep impact of those messages, but I know for sure that this was an experience that started to build my confidence as an important player in the kingdom of God on earth. The feeling behind the message sank deep within me, "Beauty is you; is around you; is All That Is!" This is a message we all need to hear. As St. Paul said in his letter to the Ephesians, "Awake O Sleeper, arise from the dead, and Christ will give you light!" (Ephes. 3:5) And until I heard this message, I really didn't realize that I was in a slumber.

I have talked with and through many others. I had a session with Kevin Ryerson, the channel in Shirley Mac-Laine's movie and book, *Out on a Limb*. Kevin channelled, verbally, John the Beloved. (Unlike Adele who brought through Spirit by table tipping—one letter at a time!) Through Claire O'Classen, St. Paul told that the duration of life on this side, as seen from the other side, was analogous to "the time it takes to get up from a chair." That had a profound impact on me as well as a few of those present at that time to help us appreciate life a little bit more. *Every moment of life is so precious!* I have also listened to Jubal, Dr. Peebles, Bashar, Sun and Moon through Gene Napol and others offer advice about finding Beauty/God in life. All of these channels had two things in common. First, they were all very kind, gentle, loving people. Secondly, their messages from spirit were filled with love, hope, encouragement and a good healthy dose of loving who you are in the eyes of God. None of the messages contained anything having "a destructive effect on the human person." They wonderfully worked "on the spiritual center of the free person," using the criteria of the theologian, Rahner, on possessions

You might be wondering about what my fellow priests were thinking about all this "New Age channeling-stuff." When I was seeing Adele and doing table tipping, one young priest pulled me aside and told me he had heard from others that I was participating in séances. He was very concerned! I told him nothing of the sort was going on and that I was only helping people deepen their relationship with Jesus and their angels. Only goodness was happening. I never heard from him about it again.

My pastor at that time, Father Kulleck, also mentioned that he had heard that some psychic stuff was going on. He told me that he had a science background (and taught science at one time in the local high school). So this psychic stuff made no sense to him and made him very nervous. "Scared" may have been the word he used. I reassured him that everything was all right and he had nothing to worry about. I would not be the cause of any scandal, so I trusted!

I was trying to explain table tipping to one of my good friends, Father Scott, and said he should give it a try. He just laughed at me and said, "I'm not gonna ask Jesus to come into a table! I can only ask him to come into the bread!" Hmmm, think about it Scott! Anyway, from that moment on, I realized it would be best not to talk about my new adventures with any of my brother priests. That included my Bishop, as I am sure he wouldn't understand either and would only be concerned about it getting into the press and causing a scandal.

My eyes, heart and Spirit leaped to new horizons as I witnessed Jacque Snyder channelling her Spiritual friend and Master Teacher, Zarathustra. I first met Jacque at Adele's house. As I have already briefly mentioned, Jacque is someone who is bound and determined to make the most out of balancing her Spiritual and human experiences. She has a clear vision that now is the time to attempt to make her human experiences, as well as ours, Spiritual experiences. We have the right, as implied in the introduction to *Star Trek* on TV, "to go where we have not gone before, to expand beyond the stuffiness and stagnation of just doing things the way they have been done for generations." With that outlook, Jacque, spiritually and emotionally, moved beyond the circle of Adele Tinning and her friends and went for herself to see what life looked like beyond and through "other windows." Her first stop was Ramtha. She checked him (and JZ Knight, the trance channel for Ramtha) out from every angle. She stepped back and from there, took off in her own direction … within. And so, after much preparation, she became a full-body channel, eyes open, of the Spiritual Master, Zarathustra. Z, as we call him. Zarathustra was/is the same physical entity (person on earth) as the man who set up the ancient religion Zoroastrianism. Since that time, he has grown and advanced to the position of a Master Teacher. The wisdom he shares with others is impeccable! His gift of communication and insight accomplishes so much in helping others realize their potential on Earth.

Under the direction and guidance of Zarathustra, Jacque set up an organization called Sacred Life Association. Sacred Life is a nonprofit organization dedicated to personal and global transformation. It desires to assist humankind with the transition to new ways to heal all of creation, including our planet Earth. Sacred Life facilitates workshops, healing and channeling sessions of Jacque and Zarathustra. One of its favorite projects is the support and integration of the spirituality and knowledge of Native Americans.

I have seen Jacque's own Spiritual growth take off in leaps and bounds. She is now able to go within herself and share her own personal wisdom and insights in order to help facilitate growth in others. Both she and Zarathustra believe in the G.U.R.U. concept. They refocus the spotlight back on you, just as God would do. I see Jacque as one who is working on becoming a Master Teacher in her own time. This transformation has been an inspiration for many of us to position ourselves in alignment with Spirit just as she has done. This process helps us all see the Beauty we are.

And so it happened: on December 28, 1991 at Jacque's house in Maple Valley, Washington. I had had a second private session with Z . During the first one, we had worked through many of the mental blocks or barriers I felt lay in my way of further aligning myself to Spirit. It was during this second session that Z told me that he was about to share information with me that would set me on a new path. I thought he was going to tell me that I was a healer and needed to use my hands more in healing people. But he didn't. Instead he told me that I was going to be a channel for a Spirit. My first dreading thought was, "Great, a Catholic priest who channels! Now I'm really going to be skating on thin ice with the church." But I immediately shifted my awareness to realize that I was/am in God's hands. My spiritual journey had been well blessed and protected from any adverse, negative criticism thus far.

So I took a deep breath and started thinking, "Hmmm, who could it be? Paul? John the Beloved? Peter? Isaiah? Who?"

"Joshua," Zarathustra spoke with a deep reverence to his voice.

"Joshua?" I asked. "You don't mean Jesus, do you?"

"But of course," he answered. "Who would be aligned better to the truths that you have come to believe and teach than the great master Jesus ... or Joshua, as they called him in his time?"

"Great, now a Catholic priest who channels JESUS! Oh well," as I have become accustomed to say when I ventured into new horizons with Spirit. "I will just take another deep breath and be attentive to what is unfolding."

"Now I am going to teach you a way to better facilitate him through this exercise you call channelling," guided Zarathustra.

I was still in a state of shock, but listened very attentively. Z went on to teach me about the procedure (which I have already explained on page 38) that allows a clear channel for the "River of All That Is" ... God, in the form of Jesus, now known as my friend, Joshua, to speak through me. (Zarathustra pronounced Joshua's name with a "Y." When I asked Joshua to spell it out, he used a "J." But it is not pronounced like the "J"oshua of the Old Testament.)

In the beginning, as I attempted to channel Joshua, I found that it was a bit frustrating because it wasn't like Jacque and Zarathustra or even White Eagle or my Tibetan Monk friend. There was no memory loss of what happened during the sessions. There was no dramatic leaving of the body and coming back, or not remembering a thing. There was no dramatic change in voice ... in fact there was no voice in the beginning ... there was simply and gently a peace beyond that which I had ever felt (and I have felt some pretty deep peace in the past!). Up to this point, I still had no reason to question whether it was Jesus or not.

But one day, a month or two later, came the same words which Jesus spoke after his death and resurrection. They rang clear in my ears: "Peace, I leave with you. My peace, I give to you." As the days and months unfolded, the voice came (a guttural, gravelly voice), the gestures came (the scratching of an imaginary beard), and the wisdom was shared. The Beauty was felt.

Many of you will be wondering if I tested this Spirit to see if it was really Jesus. Yes and no would be my answer. After I said my prayer to welcome Joshua in, I would have to say that I knew, just by feeling this peaceful presence, that I was dealing with a Christed-being. I worked with this peaceful presence for quite some time before he spoke through me. Never did I have an upset stomach feeling. Never did I sense the presence of evil. There was no "hair up the back of my neck" feeling at all, ever! Only peace.

Despite my frustrations about him not speaking immediately through me yet, I trusted that adjustments in our frequencies were taking place of some reason which he knew better than I. When he finally did speak through me (or maybe I finally allowed myself to step aside enough for him to speak through me), my first question to him was not, "Are you Jesus Christ the Son of God?" My gut reaction was that that would have been rude and disrespectful after all the progress we had made in coming to peace with one another vibrationally. Yes, eventually, he did say that he was the son of God ... but so am I and so are you, a son and daughter of God. I intend to publish another book of the dialogs of Joshua which have since ensued. This subject of who he is and who we are is gone into in great detail. He has asked that I entitled this book, *Back to Basics*. But suffice it to say, I have never had any doubts that this was not some aspect of the Jesus of Nazareth that walked the Earth almost 2,000 years ago. And all this doesn't amaze me, for as Christians, as Catholics, I would presume that we have the right to dialogue with Jesus.

In the conversations which I had (and have), I allowed the distance between us to be much closer, if not, nonexistent. That is what channeling is all about. However, one thing that always puzzled me was that I was usually aware of what was going on in a session when I channeled for others (which I didn't do that often yet). Most certainly, I was aware of all that was going on when I channeled Joshua in the car. **The car!!!!!!** You see, I had/have this bad habit (not really a bad one ... maybe impractical) of channeling Joshua in the car when I am travelling from one end of the city to the other. There, in the car, I can be away from phones, television, computers and doorbells. It allows me to be less distracted, to turn off the mind-chatter a wee bit more and place trust in my years of experience of driving. It is strange, to say the least! (I don't think Joshua has a California drivers' license!) I go through my ritual of calling forth Joshua and then put the driving on automatic, a manner with which we all are so familiar. Joshua comes in through a deep breath, readjusts my body (keeps my eyes on the road, thank God!) and props one foot up on the seat adjuster. He usually begins with, "My beloved Patrick" or "My beloved brother, what an honor it is to be here with you." And then the wisdom pours forth. I guess it is only logical that I am present and aware of what is going on and not off somewhere in the ethers when I am channeling Joshua. After all, in most cases, the information is for me ... who better to be present!

I should also say that I have become more comfortable with not always going through the structured ritual to bring forth a verbal channel. At times, when I am sitting before my computer, I just say a short prayer like, "Okay, Joshua, I need some help in this homily or on this portion of the book or on this lesson." Then I listen to the train of thought, knowing that it is not me and trusting that it is Joshua. I put down on paper what I hear. I also do this sometimes from the pulpit and allow my mouth to speak before I can get in the analysis. But I have less confidence in my keeping my own agenda out of the way than when I am in a more controlled environment and follow the ritual of stepping aside and allowing a clear channelled message to come through. The point I wish to make is that I am usually aware of what is going on when I channel Joshua for others. But this information for others is like teflon! It doesn't stick in my mind and I'm not regulating or monitoring what Joshua is saying. I am more of a silent observer, not thinking about or judging the dialog. It usually isn't until hours later that I start to recall portions of the conversations. After that, I have found that I quickly forget most of it. I do, however, seem to be able to share in, and keep passages of, wisdom and insight for general personal growth for myself and others. For that remembrance, I am thankful.

I have become very bold lately. I open up and say more to the people in the congregation, the students in my classroom, or on retreat. I tell them that I hear this little voice telling me this or that. I'm sure some have thought me crazy. Then when I tell them that I have come to believe that this voice is Jesus, the situation suddenly becomes shrouded with a bit of reverence and respect. I must say that reverence and respect are not what I am attempting to get from people, for I have come to know that this is from above and needs no confirmation. Again and again, I am asked, "How do you know it is Jesus?" Well, I am sure there are exercises you can do to tell if it is just plain old you (but remember, you "ain't" so plain and must come to trust yourself in Spiritual matters just as much as you would trust Jesus. After all, he did say, "Anything I can do, so too can you). One such exercise might be for you to think of a list of groceries that you need. Go over this list of ten-or-so items, and hear yourself repeat the words in your mind. Feel what it sounds like. I am sure it will sound quite obvious that it is you repeating the list. (It is you!) Now, take a few deep breaths and quiet down. Ask within what Jesus says (not said!) about how we are to treat one another. The answer is to be in the third person, his voice, as if he were saying how to treat others. You may at first intercede with your own somewhat rote answers (*e.g.*, "Love one another."). But allow yourself to step back and hear an answer from his perspective, his voice. If you catch yourself using an "I" statement (*e.g.*, "I am supposed to ..."), stop and let him slip in, once again using his voice, such as, "My beloved, you are to treat others as though they are me."

You should be able to note a different quality, flow or rhythm about the response that does not sound like a usual response from you. This response from Jesus/Joshua should be obviously different. If it isn't, and you are sure that it is **just** you, take more time to quiet down, breathe more, relax. You will see a difference, no ... the bottom line is that you will "**feel**" a difference and will "**feel different**" within. That is the measuring stick.

Another measuring device is the quality of the message you receive. Most of the times when I am channeling for myself, I am stressed out over some situation in life. The help and assurances from Joshua are unbelievable. Usually, by the time I have reached my destination or finished with my meditation, I am at peace and back on the right track. I feel centered and grounded in a new way that goes far beyond a simple pep talk to myself. I remember one time having a dialog with Joshua in the car. (When we dialog back and forth, he always says how much he loves to hear the sweet, dulcet tones of my voice ... and I hope one day you can hear that too about you!) Anyway, we were talking about some harsh words that someone had said to me. I heard Joshua ask me if I knew where the hurt came from? "Sure, sure," I said, "Somewhere in my childhood, and I am reacting now as if it were my dad scolding me or talking harshly, saying I'm a bad boy!" "Maybe," he said. "But let's try another way to look at it. Let's try an exercise." "Okay, buddy," I said, driving 55+ m.p.h. down the highway!

Joshua said, "Try to remember, again, the situation when your friend said something hurtful. Now instead of trying to analyze where the hurt came from, take a moment to feel that hurt." So I did. I felt it deep within me. "Now that you have **felt it**, go back to a time you associate with or remember **feeling** that same way and **feel** it again" It turned out to be a childhood situation similar to the one I had associated it with on my first guess, but this time I wasn't using my intellect, I was **feeling** it! "Good," Joshua said. "Now what does that feeling mean to you?" I felt that it meant I **was** bad, disgraced for thinking, saying or doing the wrong thing ... unloved.

"Okay," he said, "Now I am going to teach you a few things that you already know, but seem to have forgotten. My father, our God, loves you unconditionally. That love cannot diminish in our eyes regardless of what you do. You do remember the prodigal-son story, don't you? So when you think you are bad to the bone, as you say, nothing could be further from the truth. We love you. You, as a human being on the road to perfection, will make mistakes from time to time. But you are simply missing the mark and should not, will not, be condemned or made to feel bad when you err. This is our truth. It may not be your father's truth, your mother's truth or even your friend's truth. But it is our truth ... and this truth shall set you free. Now, Patrick, comes the most important part of the lesson. What do you **feel** when I tell you these truths?" I responded that I felt joy, peace, harmony, and atonement, that is, at-one-ment. "Exactly, Patrick!" Jesus affirmed. "Now, take a moment to feel these positive feelings a bit longer in the depths of your being. Absorb them! Integrate them into your being! It is the deep feeling of them that will free you from your trap." And so I did, and as I did, I began to cry and smile and laugh and feel totally uplifted. "The final important part of this exercise is to integrate into your being these new affirmations to replace the garbage that got you stuck in the first place." So he proceeded to have me repeat loving affirmations about myself and my relationship with God. Again, I felt joy and peace. It was the feeling and the quality of the message and the results it produced that made me certain of the messenger.

Here is another example to illustrate that the quality of the message lends credence to the proof of a qualified messenger. Sometimes the message is not always one that I would like to hear. I want "my" truth to be verified. One time, a young friend of mine had just died. I was still very angry and upset and wanted to know why Jesus didn't bring him back from the dead as he did with his friend, Lazarus. Gently, he told me that the purpose of bringing back Lazarus from the dead was to show people that death was not a permanent end. Many people believed, in the day of Jesus, that you simply ceased to exist when you died or went to a place of nothingness, far different from our eternal concept of heaven. Jesus wanted to show, then, that the Spirit or soul did continue and was not terminated or obliterated, so to speak.

"So!" I said, still very angrily, "You could still have brought him back and prevented him from dying! He was so young!"

"Patrick," he softly spoke, "Have you forgotten about the reason of my death? I died and rose from the dead to show you that life continues on in a new form, a Spiritual form. And don't you remember that I told my disciples, 'In my Father's house are many mansions. Otherwise, how could I say I was going to prepare a place for you?' Life is everlasting. Your friend transformed. He is here with you. All physical bodies grow old and die in their own time. But you, my friend, know and need to continue to believe and teach that life, as the Spirit and soul know it, continues on in the Kingdom of my Father in heaven."

"Oh," I simply said with a sigh that felt as though the weight of the world had just been lifted off my shoulder. The quality of that message at that time of my distress could not have been from anyone but Jesus!

Are you really Catholic, Father?

I'm sure even Jesus was asked the question, "Are you really Jewish, Joshua?" No doubt after having read the last section on channelling, I'm sure there are some (hopefully not many!) who are wondering how I can believe in all this. If you are, you are not alone! I remember one night, one of my best priest-friends and I were having a discussion over some problems in my life. I was sharing with him my metaphysical perspectives on these issues. After a while, a perturbed look came to his face and he said, "Why don't you stick to your own traditions. They are so rich with information. Why don't you offer these struggles up to God!?!" That was just like telling me, "Hey, it's okay to suffer! Don't try to get over or through it. There must be a reason and you will discover it when you get to heaven! Don't try to work through these issues using a direct line to Spirit, now!" He may not have said exactly that ... but that was the gist I got from him! In thinking about channelling, I believe one of the reasons it is possible is because I know God is a part of everything and everybody. Therefore, we should be in intimate contact and conversation with God, with Beauty, at all times. Channelling is one of these connections.

I was talking another night with Father Chuck, a next-door-neighbor at the rectory. I was sharing with him my thoughts on channelling. In his best New York accent, he said, "Pat, are ya nuts? God can't speak to you in words. Let me tell you how he does it. You see, when I want to know something from God, I go for a walk on the beach. Thinking about my problem, I sense when God and I are one with a particular answer. But he doesn't say, 'Hey, Chuck, you should do this or that!' You're nuts Pat!" Hmmm, maybe I missed something in the Bible. I thought it said, "Speak Lord, I'm listening" ... not "Make me sense you Lord!" (Not that you can't do that also!)

Another time, I was having lunch with a very scholarly Monsignor, and again, I directed the conversation to channelling and the subject of metaphysics. I said that God is in everyone and we can tap into God in many ways. "Dear Patrick," the good Monsignor chided, "where did you go to the seminary? Didn't they teach you that that is Pantheism? Don't you know that that is a heresy?" Hmmm, again. Excuse me, Monsignor, but what seminary did you experience God in?

None of these conversations sent me into a deep, soul-searching journey. As I have said before, I just believed that it was so natural to talk with God and/or Spirit this way. So, *no offense* Chuck, Monsignor or my best buddy, but you are limiting God. John Michael Talbot, a singer and recording artist, says in one song, "My Hands Belong To You," that whenever we say we will work for the Lord in all areas *"except ...,"* then we are limiting the full working of the Spirit of God in our lives. For those of you who are having less difficulty with the subject of channelling and are willing to challenge yourselves to find new ways that the Lord can work through you to build the Kingdom of God on earth, then I encourage you to confidently take some quiet time to hear the Lord and all his mighty angels place his words down deep inside of you without placing any *"excepting"* conditions on it. Go one step further and give yourself the courage, honor and privilege to voice those words. In doing so, you will experience a profound peace and find that there is hope in and for this world.

In another part of this book, I mention that I went to the shrine of Our Lady of Guadalupe in Mexico City. When I knelt before the altar, Jesus came to me and told me how much he loved me. More importantly, he told me to tell the people, especially the people of my parish, that he loved them all very much. People of faith, people of any faith in God, believe me: in all the channeling sessions I have heard or spoken, I have never heard a harsh or bitter word from Jesus or any of his angel Master Teachers. I have only heard words of support, love, encouragement, guidance and wisdom.

When I was up in Canada for "The Gathering of The Four Races" (see Chapter 6), a great Spiritual Master came to me in meditation. He told me it was "time to come out of the wilderness." This message, I believe, is also for the rest of the world. This world is in such desperate need of a healing, and in need of an awakening in remembrance of who we are. This is the Kingdom of God on Earth that was given to us to steward and shepherd. Somewhere we lost our way. Maybe, just maybe, we weren't listening to the right voices, to the voice of God and those who come in his name. Now is the time for us to prepare the way of the Spirit of God in all our hearts by opening pathways, new roads, avenues, rivers, yes, even new channels to allow God's love and guidance and presence to bring about the Kingdom of God on earth as it is in heaven.

One more angel ... I mean, angle!

I have always had trouble satisfactorily defining the term *metaphysical.* I used to think it meant "beyond the physical," ... that which the scientist could not prove: Spirit. I'll still go with that definition when I try to explain to you another aspect of channelling which you may find comfortable and not so threatening. Maybe intimidating would be a better word because many people find it hard to accept the fact that Jesus or any saint or Spirit would speak through *them.* I would like to let you know that there is another source that you can tap into and that source is **YOU**. You may remember an old analogy of God used in the Baltimore Catechism. It said that God, Jesus and the Holy Spirit were like steam, water and ice, all different vibrations but the same substance. I look at that analogy with a different twist when I think of our relationship to God. God is the fast vibration, steam. When you slow down the vibration of steam, it becomes a bit more dense and hence, water. When you really slow down that vibration, you have a solid substance, ice. Now the church would have used this analogy to show us that Jesus is the "ice" and therefore one with God. But I think you can use the same analogy for our creation. God takes a part of God's self and intends to miraculously create a solid substance, a human being, made in God's likeness ... that's you and me. Although we talk about only three stages of steam, water and ice, there are actually many, innumerable levels or vibratory rates between all of those stages. So too with us. There is God, our soul level, our Spiritual level, our "I Am" level, our "Christ" level, our mental levels, our emotional levels and our physical/psyche levels ... and much more in between. So when you are taking your quiet time, your meditations, and you wish to tap into a higher level, state your intention to open yourself only to *your higher levels*. When you hear that gentle, peaceful, wisdom-filled voice, be bold enough to ask it, in the name of Christ, to tell you its name. It must answer! Be open to the first name you receive even if it is all mumbo-gumbo to you. (Who says "they" speak English in the Spirit world? And, I am sure not everything can be translated into English as easy as we Anglos presume it can!) The next question is just as important: "Do you come in the name of the Christ (That is, one who is aligned with God and God's truth)? If it answers "no," that simply means it (or the level you have tapped into) is not yet advanced enough to understand its Chrisedtness and be on the Master level. If the answer is "no," bless it, surround it with the love of Christ and then the light of Christ and ask Jesus to take it (or you) to a higher level. In my earlier metaphysical days, through a course called *The Teachings of The Inner Christ*, I often talked to my Christ level (helping me make sense of my daily reality) and my I Am level (making sense of my relationship with God). These were all wonderful helpful messages that I could voice. Still, they were nothing compared to tapping into the angels, the Master Teachers and Jesus.

I started off this postscript with a *faux pas*, "angle, not angel." But, of course, I did it on purpose. It is my belief that angels were once humans who "got it" when they were on Earth. They made the connection with their purpose and mission on Earth. They realized their true connection with God and made their stay on Earth a paradise. Even the church labels saints like that, as having accomplished that goal. But the church usually waits until they have created a few miracles back on Earth once they have passed over to the other side. However, the church is willing to call certain people, like Mother Teresa, living saints. The goal of all of creation is to become an angel one day, to earn our wings. The major ingredient to this process is to understand and live out deeply our beautiful connection with our creator, God, our constant companion. Channelling: speaking or listening to words planted deep inside of you, is a step in the right direction. For those of you who have picked up this book and are striving to expand your relationship with God, I commend you. A word of encouragement to you, the wise: your wings, so to speak, are starting to bud. Ready yourself for a grand adventure. Soon you will feel as though you are floating and walking on air. Each day of your life, when you are in communication with the Lord or his angels, will be filled with Beauty, great insights and wisdoms. **"Speak Lord; I'm listening. Plant your words, your life, deep within me!"**

Sunday Sermons

(I have included at the end of some chapters, one or two of my past homilies (sermons) which can give you a flavor of how I worked Catholicism and New Age thought together.)

Oftentimes I have a dialog homily with God, Jesus, Mary or possibly another character from the Gospel. It livens things up. This is a good homily to place after the chapter of channelling because the subject is dealing with letting go and letting God. That is one of the first "rules" for communication with the Source. When I do these dialog homilies, I usually talk louder (or softer), deeper (or gentler) for God, and oftentimes I will be looking up when I talk with "him." When God speaks, "he" lovingly looks out at the people. In the following, I will be the bold type and God will be the italic.

God? ... I have heard this story about Jesus calming the storm so many times that I could give my sermon by heart!

Go ahead, Patrick, tell it again. I love to hear my creation interpret what I meant!

We ... I always tell them that the storm in the Gospel represents the storms in people's lives.

Oh, I like that Patrick.

Thanks God. Then I tell them that if we call on Jesus, he will tell the storm—whatever or however that is represented in one's life—to stop. How 'bout that God?

Not bad, Patrick.

Not bad! What do you want, God?

Well, you know these things down on Earth you call donuts? It's kind of like that ... you left out the middle.

Left out the Middle?!?

That's right. You have set the scene and you have interpreted correctly my natural response, but you have left out the meat of the subject. Until you can understand the meat of it all, you especially you as humans, rarely (excuse the pun) receive the benefits.

Now let me guess God, what is the main course that we are missing? I bet it is the fact that when the storm appears in a person's life, we forget to ask for your help. It that it, God?

Not at all, Patrick. In fact, the phone usually never stops ringing off the hook up here. Would you like to guess again, my little one?

Oh, you notice I have been losing weight! Sure, why not? Let's see, we do have storms in our lives; and we do ask; and I really believe that you are there for peace. ...

That's right.

Well then, I don't know what's missing.

Patrick, is there truly peace in your life? Have all the storms calmed down, knowing that I am there captaining your journey and that we can avoid all major storms? Are you at total oneness with me, your God?

Gee, God, I guess not. What's going on?

My friend, there seems to be a problem with most humans in that they are afraid to experience me and my presence at a deep level. A level which brings deep peace and contentment. They are afraid to feel that.

I don't understand that, God. Why would we be afraid to be at peace?

Oh, I know that you want peace in your life. But you want it your way. You remember that little guy named Linus from the Peanuts cartoon strip that I planted in someone's mind? You are somewhat like him. So many of you are afraid to let go of your own security blanket and let someone else be in control. That's what it would be like to have peace in your life. Let go. Walk with me to the front of your ship of life and let us sail together. If you continue to do it on your own, you will continue to often run into rough waters. But if you let me help, as the disciples were willing and even eager to do in the Gospel ... if you let me help you steer ... if you let me ...

God, are you as nice and warm and fluffy as my own security blanket?

Oh Patrick! Just let go and see for yourself.

Chapter Three
Reincarnation:
Beauty Revisited
"Not This Lifetime"

ometimes I have to laugh at myself and shake my head when I quickly come up with off-the-wall ways (albeit clever and sensitive ways!) to answer the barrage of questions that come the way of "Father Pat." When I was at Adele's house someone asked me if I, as a Catholic priest, believed in reincarnation. Right off the tongue rolled my answer, "No, not in this lifetime!" Everyone laughed and I avoided answering the question. I thought to myself, "Slick job, Patrick. Got you off the hook again from making a commitment to what you believe in." But then I started thinking maybe that answer wasn't so incorrect for ME. As a Catholic priest, I am not supposed to believe in reincarnation. The church's present teaching is very clear on the belief that this is the one and only life we have. So naturally, this lifetime, I do not believe in reincarnation. "Yeah, but what do you really believe, Father?" someone later persisted.

First of all, what does the church technically believe? As it stands now, they don't believe in reincarnation in any lifetime. This is a one shot deal, and you don't get any second tries. You find Beauty in this lifetime on earth or not! When you die, you go to heaven or hell ... or that nebulous purgatory to work off negative points until you are good enough to get to heaven. But has the church always believed this? NO! It wasn't until the Middle Ages that the church definitively said it didn't believe in reincarnation.

Before we come to that alleged conclusion, let's look at some of the preChristian, Old Testament thinking and then some of the New Testament passages. Talk of the immortal existence of the soul is rarely found in the Old Testament. The general consensus is that the Old Testament rejected any natural or innate immortality. However, some mention of the preexistence of the soul can be found in the Old Testament in the book of Jeremiah. "Before I formed you in the womb, I knew you, and before you came forth out of the womb I sanctified you and I ordained you a prophet unto the nations." (Jeremiah 1:4–5) Here we have the Lord telling us that together, we work out a plan for our Spirits to accomplish in our bodies. The Master Plan, the prophet's role which we all must play, is to remember who we are and help bring heaven onto Earth. Reincarnationists (and evidence of how our world has evolved) point to the fact that we don't usually get this right the first time and need to come back to accomplish this task, again and again. And without being so specific as to limit your role to that of a prophet, coming back is merely another experience to be a creation of God in skins to adventure (and find Beauty!) in the playground of God.

The New Testament speaks more of the possibility of reincarnation. Does it say anything directly about reincarnation? No. There is a possible anti-reincarnation statement in the letter to the Hebrews, but I shall address that in a moment. Why didn't Jesus in the Gospel or St. Paul in the other books of the New Testament say anything about reincarnation? I think the number one reason why it was not mentioned is told to us by Sylvia Cranston and Carey Williams in an excellent book, *Reincarnation, a New Hori-*

zon in Science, Religion, and Society. They emphasize the fact that "Christ's disciples expected the world to end shortly after his death. Hence there was no need to think of futures lives, which would never be lived." You see this accentuation on the end of the world-thinking in the following scripture references:

- John the Baptist said, "Repent for the kingdom of heaven is at hand" (Matt 3:2).
- Jesus told his disciples, "Preach as you go, saying 'The kingdom of heaven is at hand'" (Matt. 10:7) and "When they persecute you in one town, flee to the next, for truly, I say to you, you will not have gone through all the towns of Israel, before the Son of man comes" (Matt. 10:23).
- Jesus also predicted that the end of the world would happen with the destruction of the temple in Jerusalem (which really happened in 70 A.D.) (Matt. 24).

If the followers of Jesus took these words literally, then naturally, there wouldn't be any worry or talk about reincarnation. There would be nothing to come back to. And maybe Jesus did say something about reincarnation but the writers of the Gospels were so focused on information which pertained to the end of the world times, that they failed to write any reincarnation information down.

In the same vein, just because it wasn't mentioned in the New Testament doesn't mean that Jesus didn't talk about it or that the people didn't believe in it. There are many subjects such as the Trinity or the Virgin Birth of Mary that are not mentioned in the Bible. Yet, that does not invalidate the subject. One also needs to remember that by the time the early Christians realized that it wasn't the end of the world, as they so thought, a great time span had passed from the death of Jesus and the first written Gospel. Nearly thirty to forty years had passed. Again, thinking that the end of the world motive was the relevant focus, anything else spoken by Jesus which could shed light on this subject would have been easily forgotten forty years later. Can you remember a conversation you had 40 years ago?

I think it is important to mention *other* teachings of Jesus. The last sentence in the Gospel of John says, "There are still many other things that Jesus did, yet if they were written about in detail, I doubt there would be room enough in the entire world to hold the books to record them" (John 21:25). The Gospels also mention that Jesus had two teachings, one for the public and one for the private hearings of the disciples (Mark 4:11, 33–34). Many of the Gnostic (secret) Gospels of Jesus, as well as the Dead Sea Scrolls, deserve greater attention, for these teachings also re-enforce the belief about the rebirth of the human soul.

But there are many New Testament passages which do speak of the possibility of reincarnation. In several instances, both John the Baptist and Jesus were asked if they were the (deceased) prophet of old Elijah, who was to return. Malachi, in the Old Testament, sets the stage for these questions put to Jesus and John. "Lo, I will send you Elijah, the prophet, before the day of the Lord comes, the great and terrible day" (Malachi 3:23f.). So the Jews asked John directly, "Who are you?" and he answered, "I am not the Messiah." They questioned him further, "Who, then? Elijah?" (John 1:21). Elijah had been dead for quite some time now. Obviously, they believed in some form of a person dying and this soul returning back into a new human body.

The disciples echoed the same thinking of the times in the Gospel of Matthew. "When Jesus came to the neighborhood of Caesarea Philippe, he asked his disciples this question: 'Who do people say that the Son of Man is?' They replied, 'Some say John the Baptizer (who was beheaded and dead), others Elijah, still others Jeremiah (also dead) or one of the prophets'" (Matt. 16:13–14). Again this seems to be a confirmation of the belief system of that time. Jesus, himself, later goes on to talk about the connection between Elijah and John. The disciples were asking Jesus, "Why do the scribes claim that Elijah must come first?" Jesus told them, "Elijah will come first and restore everything. Yet why does scripture say of the Son of Man that he must suffer much and be despised? Let me assure you, Elijah has already come. They did entirely as they pleased with him, as the scriptures say of him" (Mark 9:11–13). John the Baptist was Elijah!

Another convincing argument is the discussion revolving around the blind man. "As he went on his way, Jesus saw a man blind from birth. His disciples asked him, 'Rabbi, was it his sin or that of his parents that caused him to be born blind?'" (John 9:1–3). If it had been this man's sin then it must have been from a previous life, before he was born! So this belief of reincarnation is not as foreign to Jesus and his times as we would like to deny it to be.

Finally, one of my favorite scripture passages of all time. Jesus said, "In my Father's house, there are many mansions" (John 14:2). I have used this line so often in trying to convince people about the fallacies of an eternal hell. Jesus says that he is going to prepare a place for us. I am convinced that God is not a vindictive God and therefore, if one of us makes it through this life and doesn't learn the proper lessons or treats himself, herself or others poorly, then they are still going back to the Creator, the Father's house. But they surely wouldn't be involved in the same level as, shall we say, a saint. So maybe they go to the basement, or out to another part of God's property (We must remember we are using human terms, which can't possibly come close to portraying the way it really it.). God, being the benevolent God that we know God to be, is going to want that soul to keep learning who it is and where it came from. And, to take this one step further and place it in the context of the beliefs of the times, quite possibly that "classroom" is back here on earth. What better place to continue to learn lessons that in the long run would also bring this planet back to the paradise it is supposed to be.

Some anti-reincarnationist will quote from the Epistle to Hebrews (9:27) as a standard for the "one life only" theory.

The old King James translation said, "It is appointed unto all men once to die, but after this the judgment. ..." They take this to believe that you live once and then they are judged at the final judgment. You can't live other lives before the final judgment. But the new, more scholarly, translation reads, "Just as it is appointed that men die once, and after death be judged. ..." For a reincarnationist, this means that after each life there is a judgment and then there may be another life on Earth, continuing the process.

The church's official rejection of reincarnation is based on their early rejection of some of Origen's teachings. Origen (185 A.D.–250) was one of the early church's most learned and most original thinkers of the early Christian Fathers (Where were the Church Mothers? That's another story!). He was associated with the belief of reincarnation but his main focus was on the preexistence and afterlife of the soul. Two hundred years later, some philosophers were attacking parts of Origen's belief, not specifically reincarnation. However, Origenism became a handy basket into which to throw all opinions anyone disliked. In 400, a patriarch of Alexandria called Origen the "hydra of heresies" and promised persecution of all of his followers. When the Second Council of Constantinople (the Fifth Ecumenical Council of the Church) was about to begin, another battle ensued between the Emperor Justinian and Pope Vigilius. There was rarely any talk about Origen's stand on reincarnation. Most of the struggle focused on Origen's beliefs about Monophysitism and Nestorianism (Those two terms are almost not worth looking up and deal nothing with reincarnation). Along with all this spin, there was beginning to be a schism between East and West. So Justinian elicited the East to back up his defense against Origen. The Pope vacillated, agreeing, then withdrawing support. Eventually, after the Emperor called the council (not the Pope) on May 5, 553 and the Pope refused to attend. The East won and many "anathemas" were proclaimed ... meaning, "Don't even think of reading talking or believing in such things!" However, Origen's name was only mentioned once. In any event, Origen's works all disappeared and those that remained were rewritten by his "friends" to protect him from any further heresy. His truths about reincarnation got lost in petty partisanships of ecclesiastical quarrels.

It is also interesting to note that there is some evidence that kings, queens and popes had their own personal reasons for disregarding the theory of reincarnation. Isn't it natural that a queen would not want to accept the fact that she was or could be a lowly, simple, poor peasant. Best way not to deal with that reality is push for its abolishment. Imagine the thinking of a Pope who would consider this notion when what he wants to do is make his people behave and be as good as they *"should."* Logically, he would think that his poor dumb people couldn't do that themselves without any rules and regulations. AND if they knew that they could come back another time, why, they would sin, sin, sin! The rulers of the world, the popes, kings and queens definitely would be against reincarnation.

So with this type of logic, as well as the oustings of Origen and his teachings, the medieval councils made up their minds for the people. Publicly they simply stated and assumed that reincarnation had been long-ago outlawed. They focused their attention on what they thought was important. Their belief at that time was that the soul swiftly moves at the moment of death to its final eternal resting place of either heaven or hell ... or even purgatory, where you have to work things out until you get to the point where you can enter heaven. Hmmm!

The church believes that purgatory is a place where you go if you have died in a state of grace, that is, you didn't do anything bad enough to go to hell. But you have not become perfect yet so as to enter heaven, So in purgatory, you "work off" or purify that which hasn't been cleansed through forgiveness or wasn't punished enough due to the severity of the act. (Just a personal note here. I never felt comfortable with this concept. It did not reflect my concept of an unconditionally loving God. I was always fond of saying, "Yes, there may be a process of purgation. But when I come face to face with the Light and Love of Jesus or God, I sure am going to be purged of any false beliefs I had in a second. How could anyone not be so bowled over by such love?)

When you talk about not going directly to heaven and having to work things out in purgatory, it would almost sound as though you were talking about reincarnation. Many people believe that reincarnation is a mechanism that allows a soul to purify itself from wrong doings of the past. The fullness of heaven cannot be appreciated until that purification has been completed ... which mirrors the belief of purgatory. That is, at least a foot in the door toward accepting the fact that reincarnation is a reality, a process in our attainment of heaven .

From the all evidence I have read about the scriptural references, coupled with the pre-Jesus and early church struggles, I am comfortable with the belief that reincarnation does exist. You also need to know that there is an abundance of literature out there by very reputable psychiatrists, psychotherapists and hypnotherapists (please see suggested reading list at the end of this book), which discusses the use of past-life-regression therapy and its value. Countless cases using past-life-regression have produced many cures emotionally, physically and Spiritually.

I, too, have worked with many people using this type of therapy. While studying for my Master of Arts in Counseling Psychology at the University of Santa Clara, I took a course in hypnotherapy. It was a very general, theoretical course and much of the hours of practice were left to an additional class to gain our state certification. We did talk about past-life-regressions and the value of that therapy. After that class, I began to read up on as much as possible about the value of past-life-regressions. Many noted psychiatrists such as Drs. Brian Weiss and Raymond

Moody added much to my understanding of this subject. I also took a course taught by Jacque Snyder which was bent more toward the spiritual aspects of regression therapy. Most of all, I have learned a lot by reading the works of Dolores Cannon. Dolores is a past-life-regressionist who has been doing this work since 1979. She has had fascinating experiences and, as you will see if you took at the titles of her books, has covered a wide history of past lives with her clients. Along with presenting a great deal of historical research on the time period of her client's past life, her question and answer format in her books added valuable instructional aids for my use of regression therapy with clients. As well, I have worked in this area in my own personal life. It is all very fascinating and helpful and I will discuss both areas, personal and client regressions, in this chapter.

In Chapter Four, about the pyramids outside of Mexico City, I will talk about reincarnation in the context of having been here before and lived as many people—male, female, black, red, tall, skinny, *etc.* In that context, we should realize that we need to be more compassionate with others, as we have walked in their shoes, so to speak. *In this chapter*, I focus more on the issue that because we come back again, we have to appreciate life as a gift now ... to make the most out of our journey this time, to learn, to grow, to experience life through a new perspective: To Live! And in order to live to the fullest, it may be helpful to look into past lives and how we held on to certain aspects of a past life or how we can learn from the lessons of a past life.

Let me use my own life's journey in this area as an example. For many years, I struggled with my relationship with my father ... as I am sure he did with me. One of the issues was that he always felt he had to "father me," despite my adulthood ... and that I had to "son him," always acting as though I didn't have a right to speak my mind and never disagree. From his perspective, I was not acting like a son and was always telling him what to do. I had been to

traditional therapy and made some headway but still something was missing. I went to a regression therapist and
after the normal induction, I was guided to the seat of this
issue. What I saw was an Indian village. I was the chief
and my father was my brother in this Indian village. He
also was the shaman and medicine man. The scene vividly
showed me riding into the village and coming up to my
brother's teepee. There were many braves around his
teepee, pulling him out and yelling at him for something
horrible he had done. I rode up and told the braves that this
was a private matter and should not be handled in front of
everyone to hear and see. We would handle this in the
lodge among the elders. The regressionist then asked me
to go to the next important scene. I immediately "travelled"
to a night scene outside the village. My brother was down
on his knees crying. I was telling him it would be all right.
I would handle things, being the chief of the tribe. He could
count on me to take care of him. The therapist then told me
to go to the next lifetime dealing with this relationship.
Before she could snap her fingers, I gasped and yelled,
"Wait! He's killing himself!" I was racked with emotion!
I felt so bad. So responsible.

   What the therapist and I next did was some light work.
This is a process during which you go through the death of
that particular individual. You are taken up to the light, the
Source, to God. A full spectrum lamp is used on the subject at this time. With eyes closed, it makes you feel like you
are right back home, in the Light of God. At this time, with
the help of your guides, you can review your last lifetime
and see new insights and wisdoms. What I learned from
that lifetime was that I held on to a lot of responsibility for
my brother's/dad's death. In light of that (no pun
intended), I learned that in this present life with my father,
I didn't have to be responsible for his life. I didn't have to
feel like I was the adult and he was the son. I learned, like
a light going on in my head, that this was his lifetime, it is
also mine. We both had our own lessons to learn this time

and we need not interfere with each other. Most of all, we could love each other for who we were this time and appreciate the fact that we are somehow bonded with each other in such a special way that we are back in our lives together again.

This brings me back to the reason for this chapter on reincarnation. It is to enhance life, realizing how special, how privileged it is to come back to this paradise and make it happen the right way this time. I do know that my relationship with my dad changed dramatically from that point on. Because I had a new understanding of our relationship through past-life-regression therapy and was more at peace with him. He also seemed to make some shifts in our relationship, though I did not speak to him about my sessions. Again and again, I say, God is good ... and so has my life with my father become, thanks to the belief in reincarnation.

I would like to tell you about one more wonderful past-life scenario. While I was working on obtaining my state license to become a Marriage, Family and Child counselor, I worked, in San Diego at the Christian Institute of Psychotherapy and Training. It was run by a psychologist, priest-friend of mine who has since died. Mike was a wonderful man who was very patient when it came to my New Age adventures. He listened very attentively, then would laugh and mock me with his great "Brooklyn-accented" gusto. Yet, he often brought up the subject when we were doing something other than work and, in a roundabout way, expressed interest in knowing more about his and all of humanities' relationship with God. Like so many of us, he wanted to find out if there was a another way to know more about the truth of God and life. But with regards to the clients, he warned me not to get "too heavy into it"—the New Age adventures. When I explained to him that the only area I had pursued thus far was past life regression work, he found it fascinating. But again, he strongly suggested that I not go any further than that horizon.

Regression therapy is accepted by other therapists even if they don't actually believe in past lives. I told any clients with whom I would do this type of therapy my belief system, my reality of reincarnation. I boldly stated, "I do believe in reincarnation." (Most of my clients knew I was a Catholic priest. To those that didn't, I revealed that information. I didn't wear my priest clothes in the counseling sessions.) Then I would say, "If you are having trouble accepting the reality, then go for the benefits. Many traditional therapists believe that your subconscious mind creates such past life scenarios without actually being true. But the symbolism, the benefits from that information, is important to understand present issues."

"So when regression sessions are being conducted," I continue to explain to them, "especially when a session is focusing in on a specific issue, believe that your mind, your subconscious, your Spirit and your soul are so miraculous and wonder-filled that they can help create a scenario in such a helping way that it will be beneficial for your growth. Because answers or clarifications come up in the session, part of the results will be that you will have more peace in your understanding of how you fit in in life, why you relate to others the way you do and how you know that God is active in your life." That is the goal of this chapter: **to make this lifetime more meaningful.** Often times, I tell people, it doesn't matter whether you know what your past lives were. What is important is that you appreciate this lifetime the most.

I would like to tell you about a client I worked with, whose fictitious name shall be Rose. Rose is an excellent example of how past-life scenarios can help you revitalize your life. This gentle woman was dealing with a sexual-abuse situation as a child, low self-esteem, enmeshment and separation issues with her parents. She also had a significant weight problem and was definitely frustrated with life. She wanted to lose weight and move away from home, into a healthy relationship with a man. So, she agreed to delve into the possibility of exploring past lives in attempts to get her un-stuck in life. After getting through the initial nervousness, she became a very good regression client as she was able to enter into a deep state and recall with vividness many details. In several explorations, Rose found herself in a deep dark forest. She was very afraid and was not ready to see why she was there or where the trailways lead. Eventually, after discovering other lifetimes that shed some insight into her present situation, she was more courageous and more determined to learn more for her present growth. She found herself once again in the middle of the forest and this time proceeded down the path. She said she was able to look up to the sky, but it was all dark. It was daytime, but the sky was black. Next she came to a clearing and saw before her a huge wall. She could see buildings behind it with tall smoke stacks. Dark smoke was billowing out. I then moved her to the next significant scene. This time she was in a courtyard. I asked her to describe herself and what she was wearing. She was a teenager, about sixteen. Her clothes were tattered. What little hair she had was thin and very dirty. To the left of her was a man dressed in a uniform, tall and clean. He was yelling obscenities at her. I saw her double over with emotional pain. "Why does he hate me so much? What have I done wrong? He says I am scum because of my religious faith! Where is my mother?" When asked where her mother was, she said in a whisper, "She's dead." I asked what else was happening. She described to me that she was in a line with other people in the same shape, tired, ragged and emaciated. Only she had the officer standing next to her berating her. As though a light bulb went on, she said, "Oh, I think that is Jack, my stepbrother in this present lifetime."

The line she was standing in was getting closer to the door of a tall building. She knew what was going to happen. She knew everyone was told they were going to take a shower. She also knew in her heart that they were going to die. She was happy. She wanted to be out of that horrible situation. When the door opened and they were herded in like cattle, she chose a corner to curl up in and breathed very deeply. Around her, others were screaming ... but she was quiet. Rose wanted to die, to be with her mother, to be out of hell. Slowly, she floated out of her body and into the light.

Rose learned many insights from this one session. Obviously, she was in a concentration camp and was being exterminated for being a Jew. She was constantly being told how bad she was. With this experience, she understood how this "bad girl" programming in that lifetime could have bled through to this lifetime. We did some work in the light, the stage between lifetimes. In this Light, this presence of God, she was able to reestablish who she was. Rose began to feel and know once again that she was a beautiful creation of the Light and that no other opinions of anyone else should or could influence her. It didn't matter what religion she practiced, she knew she was a good person. God and all her angels told her so. Rose had a new sparkle in her eyes and her outlook on life seemed to change dramatically. "Now, if we could just figure out this weight thing," she said as she was leaving the office.

During the next session, then, we asked her Spirit and soul to guide us to the time when she "picked up" her weight issue. The scene that came up for Rose was a long dark hallway with many doors on either side. She told me she knew she was back at the camp. Walking down the hallway, she stopped in front of one door. She was full of anger and rage. When the officer answered the door, she began to yell at him. "How could you do that to my friend! You have no right to make her go to bed with you!" She started hitting the officer on his chest. He grabbed her by her wrists and brought her close to him. "How dare you do this to me, you little Jew! I tell you what to do here. You are nothing!" She began to sink deep into the chair before me and sob. He went on to tell her that if she became his helper, he would leave her friend alone. Immediately, she agreed. From that moment on, she performed sexual favors for the officer ... whom she determined was her stepfather in her present life. She was a young virgin teenager and sex was foreign to her. It felt good, but it was also disdainful because she loathed this man. As the months wore on, she could barely get up in the morning. She began to hate herself. Her friends and family were all starving and dying around her and she was being fed and dressed better than the rest. She missed her mother who, she had learned, had died in the gas chambers. Her heart ached. One day she resolutely decided that she would take no more of this. She told the officer and he beat her severely. He called one of his guards in and "gave" her to him. He beat her some more and raped her. She was thrown back in the barracks with the others to do manual labor. This guard came to her every day and belittled her in front of everyone. Months went by and she grew thinner and weaker. It was this guard who accompanied her to the chambers for her death, a death she openly welcomed.

In the light with God (using the full spectrum lamp), she discovered that much of her weight problem was a cover up for her fear of intimacy with men. In the past life, as well as an incident in this lifetime, she was sexually abused. If she were overweight, she could shield herself from men. She also realized that she carried the starvation theme into this lifetime. So if she ate and ate, then she would never be put in the position of starving as she had been in the previous lifetime.

With these new insights, she began to tackle her weight issue in a very successful manner. She has even begun to think about relating to men in an intimate, relationship way. Because of these pearls of wisdom gained from past-life regression, her present life has taken on new meaning. She now sees the gift life is. And now, with a greater understanding of who she is in relationship to the Light, she plans on co-creating a wonderful positive ... Beauty-filled future for herself. I believe this lifetime can be a paradise for those to choose to make it so. But it does take work. Included in this work process is the discovery that past-life scenarios have an influence on this lifetime. If you can work with a past-life regressionist to discover some of these insights, more power to you! You can also buy some very helpful audio tapes that will guide you through your own past-life experience. I have done that, and the results are just as meaningful. In journeying through these past lives, you will see the creativeness of God and his copilot: you. You and God are exploring, growing, expanding and experiencing as many new horizons as possible to "live love" through life. Even more than discovering the thrill of experiencing other lifetimes, you come to realize that your present life is a gift and should be treated as such. All the people in your life, the "good ones" and the thorn in the sides, are all your friends in Spirit. Each day you wake and greet the new sunrise. You are participating in heaven on earth. With that knowledge, begin your day with the desire to make this the greatest day of your lives. To "live love" through you, with others, and in God. This is why you came back this lifetime. Not to work off some great karmic debt you owe. Not to sluff off and goof around waiting for another lifetime to get down to business. You have come back this lifetime as a Spiritual being to live in the playground of God as a human being. Love life. Love yourself. Love the God-like Spirits that we are. To life!

Chapter Four
Teotihuacan, Mexico
"When Men Become Gods"

n both 1990 and 1991, I received a Christmas card from a friend named Joanne who, years earlier, had taken me down to see Sister Sarita, the Mexican Curandera. In each of the cards, she told me that Sarita always asked about me and would love to see me. For almost two years, I failed to respond. Finally, after the New Year of '92, I stopped by to see Sarita at her home. This is a woman full of energy! She barely speaks any English and I have to try my hardest to understand what she is saying. I speak and understand some Spanish. I always joke to people in the confessional who want to go to confession in Spanish that, "I speak Spanish a little bit but I don't understand much ... but maybe that is better! God will understand and then I will forgive!"

Anyway, Sarita was very excited to see me again and we went through a ritual where she blessed me and "anointed" my hands so that I could better help and heal people. As I was leaving, she asked me if I remembered her son, Miguel. I said I vaguely remembered him. She then went on to tell me how he had been a medical doctor in Mexico City and that he had quit his practice. He was now continuing the long tradition within their family of being a Nahuál, that is, a shaman, a priest-guide and a healer. I

wasn't sure what she meant, but I experienced a sense of
excitement go through me as though I was being opened up
to another possibility of expanding my understanding of
God and myself.

So I went to, what they called, the Temple, where Sarita
and Miguel work and have their services, to see for myself
what this was all about. They had moved from the old
storefront building in which I had first met Sarita. They
bought a house in a better neighborhood and had converted
it into "The Temple of the 7th Sun." The name came out of
the histories, soon to be discussed, of the pyramids outside
of Mexico City. Without going into too much detail yet, this
"Temple" would be a new place to help people discover their
spiritual nature and that *now* (in the Seventh Sun) is the
time to do so. The house had been remodeled to better
facilitate group meetings. There were side rooms for private
healings and one large room for lectures and group
meditations.

I met Miguel, once again, and was immediately attracted
to the peaceful look within his eyes and the peace that
exuded from his heart. That night he gave a brief talk about
how we all are a part of God; that the body we inhabit is just
a shell. More importantly, he said that our brain creates a
judge and a jury that constantly puts us down and makes
us live in fear. This little judge and jury can grow and
become our whole life. It feeds on this fear it has created.
This judge, as well as ourselves, actually comes to believe
that fear and doubt are truth. All situations in life, then,
reflect that we need to be afraid of judgment. He went on
to say that we need to be constantly aware of the fact that
we separate ourselves from God; that all religions (Uh oh,
watch out, Patrick! They are treading on your territory!)
tend to perpetuate only the belief that we are less than God
and our only hope for fullness and completeness (salvation)
can be when we get to heaven. On the positive side, Miguel
said that the **only thing** we have to be concerned with is our
relationship with God. Anything else is unimportant. The

result is that everything will be important when your first priority is your communion with God. All this worry, fear and anxiety "we create" in our lives comes from a false God who says we have to be concerned about what others think and how others judge us. To deflect or defeat the judge, he suggested, we need to consider ourselves unimportant to others. The only importance we have is in relation to God! Now that made a lot of sense to me. Again, he was giving "one of those talks" about experiencing the truths of who we are that just rang so clear within me. Many people in organized religions lay guilt trips on us when we do or do not do something. Others in organized religions help us see that we "miss the mark," which is the meaning of sin, and that we need to correct our course, so to speak. Jesus was the one who said it is the relationship with the Father-God that is all important. He said, if you know him (Jesus), then you know the One who sent him (God) (John 14:7). When that becomes the most important relationship of your life, it doesn't matter what others are thinking about you. You are here to enjoy life to the fullest, trusting in your actions because they reflect your deep relationship with God and reflect the life of Jesus. If you make a "mistake," learn from it, grow, move forward and experience life in a new, fuller way. Laugh, play, celebrate ... that is what you are here for! Miguel went on to say, "If we know God through Jesus, then we are to live the way of forgiveness and love just as he lived and loved. That brings about the peace and tranquility of which Jesus spoke. A life with no fear, judge or jury ... it is all based on our relationship with, and understanding of, God."

Miguel then talked about some pyramids outside Mexico City where this process could take place at an accelerated rate. The pyramids were called Teotihuacan ...literally translated: "Where Men Become Gods." Where men (and women!) become Gods? Hey, wasn't that something I hoped for? After all, St. Paul said we are "Infants in Christ" (1 Cor. 3:1). And another time Paul says, "Perhaps you

yourselves do not realize that Christ Jesus is in you" (2 Cor.
13:5). And to be as Jesus, meant we knew we were one
with God. That is what Jesus wants of us, remembering that
he said, "Know that I am in my Father, and you in me, and
I in you" (John 14:20). Therefore, that's what God wants
of me. Didn't I want to feel more like God wanted me to
feel? Free, unconditionally loved, filled with acceptance of
myself and others? Which way to Mexico? "Slow down,
there, Patrick! What's the church going to think about all
this?," my inquiring mind wanted to know. So, back I went
to the foundation of all my searching. Is this a road similar to that on which Jesus revealed himself to his disciples
on The Way to Emmaus? Can this be a place which reveals
new perspectives of God and Jesus around us? Can Teotihuacan hold secrets of the past that are tied in with Chris-
tianity just as the sacred scriptures of old revealed a new
perspective of Jesus to the disciples on the road to Emmaus?
What surprises does Jesus have in store for me? Ah, so
there's the "hook," the justification, upon which I can go
explore a new land in search of Jesus, past, present and
forever! *Aqui, yo vengo, Mexico!* Here I come, Mexico!

Miguel, myself and ten others (sounds like the twelve
apostles!) flew into Mexico City and wound our way, via
van and taxi, through a smoggy, overcrowded city, where
everyone and everything seemed to go at a snail's pace.
Eventually, we left this second largest city in the world and
became enmeshed in a wonderfully green, sparsely popu-
lated countryside. The roads signs said, "Pyramids: 10 kilometers ... 5 kilometers ... 2 kilo..." "There they are!," a
seasoned pyramid-traveler said! I searched the horizon
and, much to my amazement, saw two small pyramids. I
was a bit disappointed because I had briefly visited these
pyramids 15 years earlier and, although I didn't really
remember much of anything, I had the impression they
were much bigger. Maybe I would find out later why they
now seemed so small. We eventually ended up at the "Club
Med" of Teotihuacan, the only decent hotel near the pyra-

mids. There was a full moon that night. I walked outside along the fenced perimeter of the pyramid complex. There was a magical, mystical presence in the crisp night air. Moonbeams danced on the edges of the dark pyramids. I could almost hear the silent, ancient voices call me to come play, come learn, come back!

The next morning, Miguel had us all up bright and early. Although we had a good breakfast, my stomach was jam-packed with butterflies. On one hand, I was anxiously wondering what I was getting myself into. On the other hand, I was excited about new discoveries in an old land. "So, here begins the journey where men become Gods," Miguel said. He wanted us to begin the journey from the moment we left the hotel. He asked us all to start shifting our consciousness and begin thinking, breathing, talking and walking Spirit ... for that is what we are and who we come from. He had us close our eyes and walk the whole mile and a half to the front gate in silence, sensing the ground talking to us and welcoming us. This was not an easy task for me, for I am a person who has constant mind-chatter of the brain. For me to quiet down, listen and not question, to sense and feel, usually takes a great deal of effort. But today, for some "unknown" reason, it was easier to do. My mind cleared as I quieted down. I began to see within my mind, Spiritual companions journeying along the road with me, almost like the two disciples on the road to Emmaus. I felt a sense of joy that they, that *we*, were going to cross over a new horizon of God. I often missed my footing and had to open my eyes to see where I was. A car (and thank God there weren't many) would come by and I would open my eyes to see by what distance my life was spared. Is that how it is in life? Do we fail to trust the path we are on? Do we often get distracted by the modern monsters of technology? "Forward, Patrick, just keep going forward!," said The Voice within me.

"From Hell to Heaven ... in a day and a half!"

When we entered the complex and went beyond the tourist trinket shops, I gained a new perspective on the pyramids of Teotihuacan. They became (and were) huge, and the distance from one end to the other was immense. The night before they looked so small from a distance. I wondered, "When we are closer to greater and grander truths about God, does reality shift and things become more lifelike?" From where I stood, it looked as though there was one long, long alleyway to the left, and at the end was situated the "smaller" of the two pyramids. The pyramid on the right was halfway down this large alley, and seemed to be twice the size of the other. Because it was early, there were not many people there. There was an air of calm and serenity. The stones appeared as though they had just been laid in place that morning, a job yet unfinished. It was almost like the workers had not yet arrived, the native Indian priests or shamans had not yet taken their place. "Over here," Miguel yelled, "We're all going to hell!"

"Oh, good God, be with me!" I silently thought and inwardly made the sign of the cross. So off to the right, away from the pyramids, we headed for some stairs which went up and then down into an arena. Then, sitting down on the top, flat area of the stairs, we looked beyond into a huge, square, sunken arena with a small pyramid on the other side.

"This is hell!," said our fearless leader. "And remember," he added, "I love you!"

We sat in silence for a few moments taking it all in. It was massive, at least the size of two and a half football fields side-by-side. Some people were wandering around in the arena aimlessly. Other people were in groups, singing or playing flutes sold to them by the numerous vendors hawking at every corner and on every hill as we approached. Still other people were very quiet and appeared to be in a very meditative state. I began to sense an uneasiness come over me. I couldn't put my finger on the reason. Maybe this queasiness was from all this talk about hell. What's the church's official view of hell? The reality of hell is stated in the Nicene Creed that Christ descended into hell for three days. The official view reflects that which is presented in the Bible, a place of for demons and the damned, filled with darkness and unquenchable fire (Matt. 5:22; 11:23, 8:12; Mark 9:43; Luke 10:15, 16:19–31; just to name a few). The Book of Revelation goes on to describe hell in a very harsh way, "If any one worships the beast or its images, or accepts its mark on his forehead or hand, he too will drink the wine of God's wrath, poured full strength into the cup of his anger. He will be tormented in burning sulphur before the holy angels and before the Lamb, and the smoke of their torment shall rise forever and ever (Rev. 14:9–10). Jesus used much of the language of the day which was from the teachings of the Jewish traditions. Judaism and the Old Testament believed in *Sheol* (only after the Babylonian captivity of the Jews in the 5th century B.C.E.; that is to say, the concept of Hell was borrowed from the Zoroastrians). This was a place where all souls resided in darkness. Later came a place called *Gehenna* where unfaithful Jews and Gentiles would go at the end of the world, after the final judgment. Just before Jesus' time, they merged these two philosophies and came to believe that *Gehenna* was not a place for future punishment, but where the damned would "burn" even before the final resurrection of the dead. (It is quite interesting to note that there really was an actual place named Gehenna on the outskirts of Jerusalem, where the towns people burnt their trash.) Theologians have argued over the years that Jesus didn't actually endorse this Judaic concept of hell, but used it only in the context of believing in the Kingdom of God or not. He was talking more or less about the *mystery* of hell versus heaven. Remembering that he said the kingdom of God lies within each person, lays the different path, a different ground work upon which the Masters at Teo looked at hell.

Miguel expounded upon that different angle. He began
to tell us about the Nahuál's version of hell. Using an old
analogy of heaven and hell—hell is anything that is not
heaven, a false God, so to speak. He explained that any
"thing," any *"one,"* any *"thought,"* any *"action"* that
does not reflect the truth of who we are (sons and daughters of God, creations and aspects of God), any of that which
perpetuates and prompts our separateness, is something
that keeps us in hell and prevents us from our divine right.
So Miguel asked us to think about the material things in our
lives that seemed to block or distract us from God, anything
physical, material or even friends/enemies, actions or
habits. We were to step down into the sunken arena and
silently walk around this vast area. When we felt moved to
do so, we were to find 10 rocks or pebbles on the ground
that represented these obstacles to God and hold them in the
palm of our hands.

Back to the pit in my stomach. As we were told to go
into the arena, "the pit" feeling remained. Now my breathing started to become more rapid. What the hell was going
on? Hmmm? By the time I descended the twelve or fifteen
stairs to the floor of the arena, I felt my eyes welling up with
tears. A few steps into the large grounds and I started sob-
bing for a few minutes. "Hey, get a grip, Patrick!," my little
voice (E.G.O.) screamed. What I actually believe was happening was that my ego (Edging God Out) was fighting to
keep control and my God-self was beginning to feel the freedom of letting go, through tears. It could be a battle through
the eyes of the E.G.O., but the God-self knew it could win.
However, the official beginning of the letting go came within
a few minutes. I continued to collect my rocks, wondering
if I would be able to hold them all in my two little hands!
Thank God we needed to only collect a representative ten!
After searching and gathering for about twenty minutes, I
headed to a square mound, "island," situated in the middle
of this large arena. "Welcome to the Island of Safety," our
waiting leader proclaimed.

So that great big sea of land around this island represented hell in our lives. It all of a sudden became so evident to me how much hell "out there" in our lives there really was and how that hell distracted us from who we are. Just think about it in terms of religion. Religion generally tells us ways or actions that help keep us in line with God. Go to Mass, say morning and evening prayers, fast, go to confession, do acts of charity. One of the problems I see about this perspective, this window to God, is that when we are not doing these actions, our focus on God is gone and then what's left to see?!? Therefore, when we are not going to Mass, *et cetera*, we become distracted by the worldly things "out there." Our perspective on life, our impeccability about who we are, gets muddled and creates hell, which is a division or a separation from our divine origins and the divinity within. Miguel said that hell is when we think that we are important because of who we are or what we own, or we have this type of job or association with this type of people. There is a bumper sticker which says, "*He who dies with the most toys,* WINS!" That is hell. Hell can also be created by the opposite outlook. Your importance, or lack of it, is at the negative end of the scale. Someone else is more important because you don't have what they have or do what they do. So now I could see why I was getting so emotional. I knew then, and know now, deep down inside, that it is not what I have or how I act that makes me important, but **Who I Am**. In the past, I created so many façades, illusions, and masks portraying who I should be for others. To hear a different truth created confusion, turmoil or maybe even tears of release.

Some say that religion is based on actions and that Spirituality is based on who we are. Now, I am not saying that my church, that the Catholic Church, doesn't talk about our relationship with God. It does. But, as in the seminary when I seemed to be distracted from the basic truths, it seem that "we" (I) have a tendency to lose our (my) focus on actions. My emotions were coming up, maybe because I realized the falseness of my beliefs in what made me important. My tears were welling up and over, maybe because I felt badly about holding on to them for so long and that I still had a tendency not to give them up. "Let go, Patrick, let go!" a divine voice nudged (pleaded) from within.

Did this island, then, represent the truth, a buoyant life jacket in the sea of hell? Is this the place where I went in the past to find some moments of peace and refuge? Sorry, Patrick, nice try, but not according to Miguel's belief system. He explained that this island was just another illusion, another false God. In this place, he told us, we believe it is okay to struggle, it is okay to be poor (or rich), it's okay not to have all that we want or it's okay to have all we want and not worry about others. I guess you could say that this is the little devil you used to see in the cartoons sitting on the shoulder saying, "It's okay to _____ (in this game you can fill in the blank with whatever you please!)." "Hmmm," I mused, "I thought this was going to be the answer to all my struggles ... an easy way out of the hell I had created in my mind, my life." But I would soon find out that the way out of hell was much more challenging, intriguing and ongoing.

Ritual has been seen throughout the ages, and still is seen by many, as a means of manifesting a certain reality. Therefore, it would make sense that Miguel would have us partake in many rituals throughout the journey of Teo (Teotihuacan). At this time, Miguel had gathered us in the center of the island, which must have been twenty feet by twenty feet. We held the rocks/obstacles in our hands and he said a prayer about the unnecessary need for these in our lives. He affirmed the truth of our divine inheritance to have nothing block our relationship with the Creator. He then asked us to release these rocks as a symbol of, and a belief in, letting go of these false Gods that we had created in our lives. To my amazement, when I let go of these rocks, a wave of energy went through me and all heaviness, all sadness, all my tears disappeared. (*There is a real temp-*

tation here to speak to "the Catholic" about how this ties into confession and the Sacrament of Reconciliation, but I will save that 'til the end of the chapter. But just a hint: the same smile I have seen on people's face after reconciliation mirrored the feeling I was now experiencing.)

"Remember," said Miguel in the same dulcet, sweet tones as before, "I love you. And ... the only way you can stay out of hell is through love. Yes, today is a good day to die ... so follow me to the Pyramid of Quetzalcoatl. I love you!" Love? Die? Quetzalcoatl, who or what is that? Almost every bone in my body wanted to scream out in fear as to what I was getting myself into. But within my heart, I swear I could feel Jesus say, "Trust."

At the opposite end of the entrance into hell was a small pyramid. I saw that there were about seventy-five steep stairs leading to the flat-surfaced top. Miguel got up from the "island in hell" and started for the pyramid; we followed ... as sheep to the slaughter. After all, he did say today was a good day to die! At the top of the platform, much to my surprise, there was a small pyramid on the other side, separated by a deep channel. This pyramid was layered with figures of Quetzalcoatl and the Smokey Mirror-God (see picture of Quetzalcoatl on page 90).

Miguel said, "This is where the journey begins of where the men become God." He explained that we chose and continue to choose to live in hell for as long as we want. We wander around aimlessly in a large space and presume there is nothing on the other side. (That would be very similar to the Old Testament's earlier concept of *Sheol,* a place where all souls go to aimlessly wander about until the final resurrection of the dead.) But the divine spark within us all, eventually pushes us or is ignited or remembers that there is more to life than the illusions we have created. This is so akin to what Jesus tells us: that we are like the lost sheep, and the master will not give up until we are found. In this scenario, through this window at Teo, it was believed that the people who were drawn to Teo in days of its incep-

QUETZALCOATL

tion, were then moved from within to ask to come out of hell. They would then go to one of the priest-guides, or Nahuáls, who had been trained in the journey, and the Nahuál would bring him or her to the top of this platform. Mesmerized by this story, I listened intently as Miguel told how the initiate, who was brought to the top only at night, would then be asked to jump off the edge as a sign of faith. Little did the initiate know that below was a channel of water. But the leap of faith was required.

"What were they supposed to be leaping into," I asked, hoping this would be *the* answer, this would be *the* door that would open up a whole new reality for me.

"Jesus," came Miguel's surprising answer, "or Quetzalcoatl, the feathered serpent." The people back in that time believed that Quetzalcoatl was love and the only way to get out of hell was by love. Love yourself as you would come to know yourself through this journey. Come to love God as you would come to know God. Are *you* ready for the journey?

So in order to die to your old self, created in hell, you had to dive into love, Jesus, Quetzalcoatl. Luckily, we only had to close our eyes and visualize ourselves diving into the channel. As I closed my eyes, I felt a freeing and exhilarating energy all around me, as though I was falling through air. In my creative imagination, I saw myself gently falling, falling, and eventually landing in the hands of God. After that mind trip, I opened my eyes to see the rest of the group, all smiling before me. They, too, had experienced freedom. We climbed back down the stairs and walked around to the back, along the bottom of the channel, to get a closer look at this beautifully decorated Pyramid of Quetzalcoatl. I silently thanked God that I lived in this time and could do the walking and not the diving, as in the past! The many Quetzalcoatl faces on this pyramid had red feathers painted around them. Miguel again told us that this represented Jesus. In fact, Miguel firmly believes that Jesus, through his divinity and divine powers, was able to come visit this part of the world. Miguel may have been talking about bilocation. This is where a person can be in two places at one time. The Catholic church considers it possible that an up-and-coming saint, Padre Pio, was able to be in two places at one time. The Mormon Church also believes that Jesus visited many civilizations upon the Earth. Among those visited was the Americas (3 Nephi 11–22). However, they believe that he came in his resurrected body, at a different time than his physical life in Israel as we know it. Whether through bilocation or a visit at another time, Miguel's belief system was that Jesus came through Spirit, in a physical body, to teach the same message of love he had taught in Israel, only through a "different window." The people, here at Teo, saw his beard as red feathers, therefore the feathered serpent. I still had a bit of trouble seeing him as a serpent, but then I heard my little voice within say, "He eats up all your fears and loves you to death!" Hey, I could handle a Jesus like that!

I was right in the middle of the channel, lying back, trying to understand this object and lesson of love. Miguel walked up to me and told me to squint my eyes. And, if I did, I could actually see Jesus's face looking up to heaven just at the exact moment he died on the cross. I did this and started to cry. Again, I heard that ever-so-familiar voice of Jesus within me say, "You see, Patrick, this is how much I love you. I love you so much that I am willing to give up my life for you! Now begin the journey of dying to that old self that won't hear my message of love for you. Die, so that you can live." I have heard that message in some form or another in many books as well as when I stood before the crucifix in a church. But for some reason, this time it seemed to resonate deep within my being. I couldn't stop crying or feeling very emotional inside. After several minutes, Miguel took some of that emotional edge off when he said that it was now time to enter the belly of the snake. "Snakes! … I hate snakes! … Snakes are my worst nightmare!"

If you will look at the layout of Teotihuacan (see layout on page 94) you will see how a two-headed snake could be drawn from one end of Teo to the other. One end of the opened-mouth snake's head would be in the arena of Hell. The mouth would be open to the Temple of Quetzalcoatl, the body would come out of Hell and run down the Avenue of the Dead. The other end of the snake's body would be half way through the Avenue of the Dead, just in front of the Pyramid of the Sun. The same type opened-mouth snake's head would be facing this pyramid.

Let me tell you something about the snake and its significance in hindsight. Let's look at Old Testament scripture-passages about the snake. As you remember so well, as the nuns told you in the classroom, or as the priests told you from the pulpit, the snake is the sign of the devil, the symbol of all evil. It was the snake, or the symbolism of the snake, that lured the pure-minded Adam and Eve away from their divine purpose of being the caretakers of the earth and the adventurers of and in life (Gen. 3). Remember: evil, or hell, is that which separates us from God and our divine right as children, sons and daughters, creations of God. So through the snake, evil came into the world. Therefore, looking through this window of Teotihuacan, going into the snake and back out of it in a reverse order, means we go back through evil to release it, to get back to our original "paradise" and purpose. It took the serpent but a moment to make Eve see everything in a new light. Going back through the snake, in a day for us, maybe years for the apprentices of the past, would now help us see God and ourselves in a new way.

In Catholic tradition, Mary is seen the person who would crush the snake and put an end to its evil ways. As you will see near the end of this chapter, Mary will again play an important role in this present day journey, in continuing to bring forth love and light and turning away "sin."

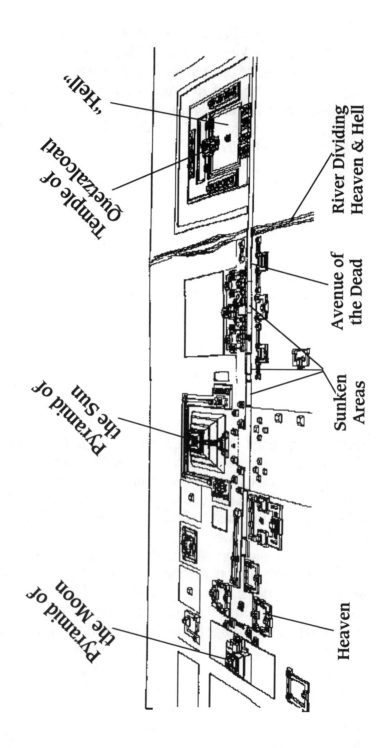

"Hell"

Temple of
Quetzalcoatl

River Dividing
Heaven & Hell

Avenue of
the Dead

Pyramid of
the Sun

Sunken
Areas

Pyramid of
the Moon

Heaven

The Belly of the Snake and
The Avenue of the Dead
~ *Rest In Peace* ~

With our new immersion into love through Jesus-Quetzalcoatl, we all were feeling much lighter. We travelled out of hell without any emotional attachments and were back at the beginning of the long corridor, looking down to the much larger pyramids. Miguel explained that this is "The Avenue of the Dead." It is down this avenue that the new students must travel in order to go through the belly of the snake, in order to die to the old self, in order to get to the other side: heaven. And so we passed over the river representing an invisible barrier which only the initiates could go beyond. This journey in the old days, although only 1,000 yards, took months, if not years. We were able to go through the stages in two days. Continuing down the avenue, we came to the first of five sunken arenas. Our teacher was sitting at the top of the stairs ready with another lesson to share with his students. "This next section represents Earth," he said. "As they tell you in the church: dust to dust, ashes to ashes. It is from the Earth that we come and it is to the Earth that we return. So now we are going to have a burial ceremony of our earthly self. It *is* a good day to die!"

In the middle of this arena was another small island, not as tall and not as smooth or worn as the one in hell. This one had a lot of small rocks and pebbles and patches of grass on top of it. Miguel gathered us in our familiar circle and talked about death. "When we die, we become Spirit. (A discussion on whether we go to "heaven or hell" was covered in the chapter on reincarnation.) We return to what we originally were. Hence the body, and all we hold it to be, becomes less important." Miguel told us to find a small stone that would represent a tombstone for ourselves. Then we were to place it in the ground somewhere and pray for our death. Miguel also told us that we could pray for, and

place in the same "tomb," any other relatives or friends who
needed to be released from any earthly bonds which held
them back from experiencing God in the fullest sense. This
sounded like what some Catholics believe about purgatory
and the need to pray for the dead so they may reach heaven.
Although I don't buy into the traditional understanding of
purgatory, I do believe that people who have crossed over
can still benefit from some light sent their way. In any
event, I chose to include my mother and a good young
friend who had just died recently of AIDS. My mom had
been dead for over 12 years and I was sure she had found
her way to the Light. Although she acted just like Edith
Bunker some times and without my dad to tell her what to
do and how to get there ... nah, I'm sure she went straight
for the Light. But I wasn't sure about my friend. Up to the
last month or two of his excruciatingly painful illness, he
had held a lot of bitterness towards himself, his God, his
church and a bit toward his family. He healed a lot of that
before his death. But if I could be of any help on his continued journey and process of growth, so be it. However, I
was mainly there for me, for my own death and my own
new life. So off I went to find my tombstone.

It was quite an eerie feeling presiding over your own
funeral. At times, my self-esteem bobs from an anchor on
the bottom of the ocean to a kite flying at its greatest
heights. To be able to stand before my grave and know that
my physical life was over, required a great deal of honest
reflection. I have presided over hundreds and hundreds of
funerals for others, including my own mom and closest relatives. What did I say there? Most of my homilies centered
around three points which were reflected in the 23rd Psalm.
First of all, I tell the people we need to remember the good
times, the "green pastures and the still waters," so to speak.
Secondly, we're not alone in the death process. I remind the
congregation that the author of the 23rd Psalm first talks to
God in the third person: "**He** guides me, **he** leads me, *etc.*"
But when the author enters into the dark valley, which

could be anything, including the death of a close friend, the author stops talking about God and starts talking to God: "Yea, though I enter the valley of darkness, I fear no evil, for **you** are at my side, with **your** rod and **your** staff, **you** anoint my head with oil, **you** set the table before my enemies." And finally I tell the people that we are *all* headed someplace eternal. "And I shall dwell in the house of the Lord for days to come." So when I stood before my own grave ... I knew that I had to accentuate the positive. All that I felt bad about, all those mistakes, guilt, remorse, misgivings, blah, blah, blah, meant nothing at this point. That was part of the purpose of this exercise: to bury all that junk and let go ... again.

The positive: What did I do in the past, what do I do now, in life that brings meaning to myself and others? When I was able to take a few moments to concentrate on these points, it brought a new vitality to life, a freeing experience, releasing some of the chains and bonds that society, church, and self place on our innermost being. This feeling may possibly be similar to those people who have experienced a near death experience [NDE]. Where they have been declared clinically dead and for some reason were brought back to life. After an encounter with the Light (God, Jesus, Mary, Buddha or some saint), there usually was a nonjudgmental review of their lives. (See references in the back of the book to Danion Brinkley's book, *Saved By The Light* and Dolores Cannon's book, *Between Death and Life* about new understandings of what happens when we die.) Then they were told that they needed to go back to resume their lives. Now the point of all this is that the person who came back was a much different person ... as though they had been born again. So, too, did I feel a new beginning as I remembered all the good in my life, past and present.

And, as I tell the people at funerals that they are not alone in this grieving process, I also did not feel alone in this ceremony. Not only were my mom and my friend there, hearing and reflecting on their own lives what was being said and growing from that wisdom, but I felt as though a whole heavenly host of angels were there saying, "Job well done, Patrick!" What an exhilarating experience ... one I wish you all—cancel that—one that I **know** you all can participate in ... but wait for the notes at the end of the chapter ... there's so much more to share!

Miguel brought me back to reality. "Now that your bones are buried, what does that leave you?"

"I know, I know," I thought, "the part that goes on to live all the days of my life in the house of the Lord!" *Not!*

"Well, you gotta wait to learn more about what is left. That's for the next section," he said. "But first I want to let you know that you are at the point of the journey where there is no return. You have now entered the belly of the snake and there is no going back. So whenever you are out there in the world and you feel you are being drawn back to hell and its evil ways, just close your eyes and come back to this grave. Remember that you are more than your skin, your bones, your physical parts. You are Spirit and you must always feel your Spiritual self. In fact, what I want you to do from this point on is to start to see yourself in and as Spirit. And as we continue to release and let go of the non-essentials, start to see your Spiritual self grow in form, walking right next to you. And remember, I love you!"

Start to see your Spiritual self grow in form? ... Now how do I do that? Jesus, are you there? Jesus? Jesus! That's the answer again. It all seems so simple when we turn to him for an example. I go back then to the time when Jesus was his Spiritual self after the Crucifixion. I do have a non-solid example to follow. Jesus was able to walk through walls in his Spiritual self. So I started to see a reflection of myself, a Spiritual self of me, walking next to me. It was less dense, almost transparent. It was more positively focused, with less negativity hanging on. After all, the past is now dead. "Let's go my friends, we have a lot more dying to do today!"

Opening The Window Of The Mind

The mind is such a wonderful, yet dangerous, creation. Just as the body gets polluted with toxins and junk, so does the mind. In following the Masters of the Toltec way, the next section of Teotihuacan was laid out so you could clear the mind. This was very similar to being in hell, but this time there was no "physical" exercise that we performed to rid ourselves of this junk. As we climbed the stone wall divider between sunken arenas, we could see Miguel sitting on the edge looking into a new arena. "So this is where you die to the monster you have created in the mind. As I have mentioned before: fear, the judge and the jury, has created many illusions and lies within your mind. Now is the time to tell them that they are no longer in control. You are no longer fighting the fight. Make them your friends." Now that was a real strange concept to me. I have always considered my mind my greatest enemy! It is quicker than lightening to judge that I am not doing something right, that I "should" be doing better, more, faster, and on and on. It's a constant battle. What Miguel was saying made a lot of sense. If I (if you) surrender and give up the fight, then the enemy is no longer able to wage war. If I can tell my mind that what it is doing is not a judgment, not a put-down, not a doubt, but that it is just one of my friends (wearing a mask of my parent, my church, my elders, my parishioners, my peers, my society), then I don't have to listen to the mind with such an emotional charge attached to it. This negatively, emotionally charged mind would normally put me (down) in place, or humiliate me, or crush my Spirit. In cleansing our minds of these false masks (or seeing them as just masks), then we can learn one of the ultimate lessons of "This Way": to listen only to the voice of the one true good Creator God within us ... the God of love and compassion and understanding. We can then see everything, every situation, as a lesson for growth.

Miguel also told us that this arena represented all the

water of the earth. It was as though the water of the Earth held the consciousness of the people. So we proceeded forward across the grass, he asked that we pray not only for a cleansing of our minds, but also for the waters of the Earth, which have been polluted throughout the world due to the garbage, our garbage, we feed it. We then set off, almost as though we were swimming through the air. But this time we had the intention of cleansing and clearing the mind. It didn't take any magic act, or chants, or prayers (although each beginning before an arena was basically started with a prayer-like, prayerful talk as an introduction). I have so many times heard my friend, Jacque and her Spirit guide, Zarathustra, say, "Belief is the doorway to reality." So I was ready to open my mind and say to it, "Come on out and play! Be free! Give up the battle! I give up, you win (ha! ha! ... we all win in this game!)." I then felt a breeze gently blow around me as I walked 50 yards through the arena. I knew this to be the Holy Spirit, the Breath of God, helping transmute my enemies into friends.

When I reached the other end, I saw that the "old-timers," those who were on their second, third or their umpteenth trip to Teo with Miguel, were smiling and buzzing about something upcoming. What more could I be getting myself into now that I had released my body, my mind? What could be left? "Hey, Mind! Stop that worrying! I am not afraid! I see life, and this segment of it, as an adventure. I am willing to learn from whatever I encounter." Yea, right, Patrick! What is the one area most people, (including myself!), *most Catholic people*, feel ill at ease with? Read on ... if you haven't figured it out yet!

"Okay my friends, now we are going to touch the heart of your soul. This next area is represented by air and we are going to let the air purify all the rest of the junk in our lives so that we can get to the soul, the essence of who we are. One of the greatest obstacles that blocks us from being who we are is SEX!" Dag nab it! I knew that that was going to be discussed sometime on this journey. When he had earlier mentioned the belly of the snake, I flashed back to the Garden of Eden story. The image of the serpent in the ancient Near East often stressed the notion of fertility and therefore sex.

I would agree with Miguel and many other people that we, as societies and/or religions, get too hung up on sex. This discussion does not imply that it is okay to go out and be as wild as possible and as irreverent of others as one could be. What *was* being discussed was the labels and rigid ideas that were placed in our minds or upon our actions ... actions which we perpetrated or were perpetrated upon us. Just think about it ... what does the church say? No, just go within yourself and think about what you are most ashamed of? Guys, was it a time you engaged in the act of sexual intercourse outside of marriage or before marriage? Women, was it the same for you or was it a time when someone improperly abused you, but you took it upon *yourself* to feel guilty? Was it something, anything, that you confessed once or twice or hundreds of times and still felt bad to the bone? What happened to God's unconditional love? Even as much as I believe in that eternal love, I sometimes have difficulty not feeling ashamed or less than perfect, which is a way, the way, so many of us think we have to be.

I have heard so many confessions that center around sexual issues. They fail to focus on God, the Father, who loves the prodigal son or daughter, without even asking what they did. Go and read Luke 15:11–24. Live that beautiful story. The son (or daughter) decided to go off and experience life in a way that wasn't necessarily true to their path. They wasted money, over drank and abused their bodies and others. Finally, they realized that they needed to be with the father, the parent figure, in their life. When they came back, face to face with their father, he didn't castigate them, he didn't question them, he didn't shame them. He welcomed them home and said, "I love you ... Now let's start celebrating life ... A party is ready for you." That implies that you are to forget about the past. It's over! Obviously, the son/daughter learned enough to move out of the past and not get stuck in it. It appears they didn't obsess about the fact that they had done something wrong, gone "off-course," so to speak. The focus was and is love, acceptance, forgiveness ... not guilt, shame and "you have to work it off until the father will let you back in."

I'd like to tell you about a confession I heard from a high school student to get across the point of how hung up people get on sin, or missing the mark, as sin means. This one young man had just been to receive the Sacrament of Reconciliation five days earlier. He wanted to go to confession again because he had masturbated twice since then and felt bad about it. Now this is one of the finest young men in the high school that I have ever met. I think he would make an excellent priest as he is compassionate, nonjudgmental and accepting of others where they are. But he thinks that his relationship with God is effected by the fact that he masturbated twice in five days!

Here's the story line I gave him. "Cup your hands together. Look at the area they cover. Let's say that represents our universe. All our planets and moons! And in the middle of your hands somewhere, there is our planet earth. Now within that area, probably about the size of a molecule, if not much smaller, is San Diego, California. And way deep within that atom is you. Now ... imagine all this space in this four by six room in which we are sitting and let that represent all the galaxies and universes outside of and beyond our own universe. Then ... think of the space of the building that this room is in and think about it in comparison to you on or in that tiny atom in your hand. Massive isn't it? Extend the space beyond the building and go way out into the street. And just think, this 'space' out there goes beyond the street, the city, the state ... and remember it goes on forever! —— And you think God is worried whether you masturbated twice last week? God is interested in all the good things you did and all the love you shared with your family and friends." "In fact," I went on to emphasize, "I think it is an insult (no guilt intended) to God if we create a God who only focuses on the bad things we think we do ... or to hold on to guilt after God overlooks our mistakes as the father did for the prodigal son. The father, God, the Creator, wants us to move on into the celebration of life, not to get stuck in the stagnation of guilt and fear."

But wait! Just to make sure you aren't getting the wrong message. Let me make certain you aren't hearing that I am saying it is okay to go out and be wild and carefree and abuse or be dysfunctionally self-centered (whatever negative stuff that includes). What we're trying to get rid of here is not only all the "crap" or negative energy that is attached to **past abuses** which prevents us from moving on, but also to get rid of that negative energy we put on some acts we continue to do which have been labeled as "evil." We must place these actions into a better light which will prevent them from being laden with a strong negative charge. This is not a rally for free sex! It is a rally for a healthy attitude about sexual activity.

And so with that dissertation in mind, our entourage moved into this next arena. A specially energized spot, a large rock, was found within this sunken arena, upon which each of us would sit to take our turn to release our pain, shame or guilt which we had carried throughout the years. We all gathered in a circle of love, around each individual doing the releasing. It was through the belief system of Teo and the help of the Nahuál, that we were able to take time to cry, sigh, or scream out everything we had held within for so many years. Miguel was able to somehow tap into our lives and amazingly bring up past issues which needed healing. I know that it took me two trips to Teo to really release some deep-seeded junk that I had held on to for so long. For some people it was easier. Others I knew, would be back to cleanse and purify completely. (Just a brief note should be said about confidences. Although no one would be put on the spot about a present or a past issue they were working on, Miguel's understanding, which made sense, is that no one needs to worry about what the other person thinks. It is only between you and God what is important in life. As said before, once *that* relationship is righted, all will flow within and through yourself and others.)

Now that we had cleansed the air and our souls felt so much freer, it was time to move on. The next realization would be like a baptism by fire, where we would be "born anew" even to a greater extent than ever before. In this next stretch of land we would be asked to recall that we had all been here before. This is very similar to the section on reincarnation but I will try to put it in a different light. Even if you don't buy into the idea of reincarnation, just the concept alone will help you understand the nature of recollecting. **Remember what this journey to Teotihuacan is all about?** Remember what the name means? "When Men/Women become Gods." The intent is to rid ourselves of our judges and juries which make us feel "less-than" in comparison to God, to others and to our own self. So let's see how the concept or the actuality of reincarnation can help us do that. If and when you realize that you have been here many times, you will see many different facets or windows through which your soul has looked. You have been male, female, tall and short. You have been white, yellow, brown and red and all the shades in between. You have been African, Asian and European. You were a slave man and a rich woman. You were as though on a lifetime of vacation and you, at one time, worked your fingers to the bone. You once lived to a ripe old age, or you have been a parent who watched all their children die at infancy. You were deformed with severe handicaps and you have been in excellent, tip-top shape. Think of the actuality of you being a criminal accused of the most grievous, imaginable crime, or you were the corrupt inquisitor, judging and condemning the innocent to death. You have been on the side of governments and you have been a rebel struggling for your rights against oppressive governments. You have been your worst nightmares and you have been your greatest dreams. Jesus said you are to love your enemy as yourself. That is reflecting the belief that we can be or were all people through the eyes of God and we are to love all aspects of self and God. When you realize that you have walked miles, lifetimes, in the shoes of so many people, you can no longer be a judge or a jury of yourself or others. When you have re-collected all that you have been and can be, you free yourself from the chains and the bonds, the barriers, obstacles and the limitations you place on your potential. You become the true Spirit that experiences a human existence. As has been said by many a great master, "We are not human beings in search of a Spiritual experience, we are Spiritual beings in search of a human experience." So why limit yourself to one form of human being? Allow yourself the freedom to share in the unlimited, as God created you to be.

No longer did we necessarily need to continue to create a Spirit double as we were asked to do several arenas past. We could now see the Spirit that God intended us to be, and not be distracted by the shell or mask which we embody. At that point in the journey, I felt like I was walking on air. I could mirror my Spirit next to me and walk hand-in-hand, or I could merge and join in wholeness with the Holy Spirit and be in holy communion with God, as God and I were intended to be. This brought us out of the belly of the snake, out of the dark night, and brought us right before the massive Pyramid of the Sun. But before we ascended this great pyramid, Miguel had us walk down the rest of the corridor to visit "heaven" and the Pyramid of the Moon.

Picture, if you will, a warm blustery night as you sit in a quiet space watching a full moon rise in all its glory. Do you remember pondering at one stage in your life how that moon gets so-o-o bright? Do you possibly remember some wise soul explaining to you that it is the sun shining on its surface from afar? Now that we have been around the world, around and through our several lifetimes and come out from the darkness of the belly of the snake, we have an opportunity to allow the sun/son to shine upon us and allow us to revel in our glory. And so it was with the men and women in the days of old standing before the Toltec Masters and teachers in front of the Pyramid of the Moon. When they had finally completed the journey, which could have taken months, if not years, they were brought before the Pyramid of the Moon to be honored before their guides. They were allowed to shine in their growth and purity, in the completion of the toughest part of the journey. They were able, through the acclamation of the hundreds gathered around them, to sluff off any last remaining doubts or hesitations which they had about their earthly selves. To an extent, they would sacrifice and release any vestige of their old selves and accept their true roles as people "who had become God." The roars of acclamation and the thunderous applause rang in our ears, too, as though we were surrounded by thousands who had gone before us.

A Little Slice of Heaven

In the last paragraph I wrote, "we have an opportunity to allow the sun/son to shine upon us and allow us to revel in our glory." The reason I used the word "son" is due to our next side-excursion, where Miguel took us to a place he called *Heaven*. Here, he believed, housed the Masters of Masters who came to teach, guide and support the Toltec teachers in their quest to help change others back to their true selves. Thus was this building called heaven.

It is very similar to the Spiritual place where we all will gather one day to continue to grow and learn and explore new horizons. The Old Testament saw heaven as the dwelling place of God. In the New Testament, heaven is where Jesus came from (Matt. 3:16) and where he went back to, to prepare a place for his followers (John 14:3). In that same chapter of John's Gospel, Jesus also tells us, "In my Father's house there are many dwelling places" (John 14:2). We also know from scripture that there will, one day, be a new heaven and a new earth (2 Peter 3:13). And, as I have tried to show throughout this book, God will be (and is!) all in all (1 Cor. 15:28).

The church uses a bit more technical language when it talks about heaven. Again, in the *Encyclopedia of Theology, the Concise Sacramentum Mundi*, Karl Rahner says:

> It is only as members of the Mystical Body of Christ that we can die in Christ; hence it is only as such that we can enter the state of heavenly glory. Thus we conceive heaven as the state of happiness that brings full, lasting satisfaction to the whole of our being through our union with the Holy Trinity in Christ together with all members of His Mystical Body.

Even I am not sure I understand all that language. What I do understand is that it is through the wisdoms and truths of Christ (Jesus) that we shall know heaven. "Christ is the final temple, heaven its sanctuary in which God is perfectly adored" (Rahner). Remember that connection with Jesus, it became very significant as we entered this temple.

The most important part of this building is in the downstairs area. The original paint and colors appear as fresh as though they were brushed just yesterday. A bird eating grain, a snail crawling along ... a sun burning in the sky. And in the center of the room there was a doorway arched into the wall which seemed to be shrouded in reverence and holiness. Many people stood before it mesmerized as though the most holy of Holies was going to walk through at any moment. Others whisked by without paying a bit of attention. Of course, it must all go back to their belief system. Just then, Miguel came over and asked me to stand directly in front of "the portal," as he called it. "This is the passageway between times, lands and universes," he whispered in my ear with deep reverence. "Here, the Master Jesus passed through many times, to be and to live with the Toltec people ... to help them get out of hell and have heaven on earth. Just close your eyes and see what comes up for you." Quietly ... eyes closed ... I melted back into the wall ... seeing the portal in my minds eye as clearly as though my eyes were open. Darkness and a black void filled the space beyond the portal. Slowly and eerily, my skin started to tingle. I began to "see" a spiritual, white, milky substance flow in the middle of the doorway. The shape of a person wearing a white robe began to take form. Then a perfect image of Jesus appeared before me. I was now one of those mesmerized, standing awestruck before what others saw as an empty doorway. At first, no words were spoken to me, but it felt as though his Spirit stretched for miles and miles of light years behind him. They stretched forth right into me. Then I heard the familiar voice. Again, it was gentle and compassionate, speaking like a mother to a son, "Patrick, I have passed through this portal countless times to be with and to help the people of this land. I now stand before you, to be with you in your search and quest for who you truly are. Be one with me." In an instant, I felt the energy which I described as coming from him to me, draw me right to him. His body and my body merged to become one between the doorway. I then felt a whoosh and I was out in the middle of the universe surrounded by all its billions and billions of stars. I was free-floating in the womb of All That Is. Jesus's voice continued, "I will come from anywhere and go anywhere to be with you, Patrick. Never forget this." In another instant, I was back, fully in my body, leaning up against the old wall. There were warm tears running down my face. I felt a peace ... the same inner peace which all in the universe must feel when it knows it is one with God. I knew this is what heaven would be like ... could be like, right now, on Earth. "My kingdom come, my will be done, on earth as it is in heaven." I looked around and my journeying party had moved on outside. We must be coming to the end of our journey, for all that was left was the Pyramid of the Sun. It was the biggest pyramid I had ever seen. How the heck was I going to make it up to the top?

"Step by Step, we will heal ..."

Step by step, there must have been thousands of them, we edged our way to the top of the Pyramid of the Sun. All the old timers seemed to be floating up on air with an sense of excitement. Finally, we reached the top and were treated to a magnificent view. We could see where we had come from: Hell, and where the journey through the snake had taken us: to the Pyramid of the Moon; and to the left, ah, Heaven! How could I experience anything greater? "Okay, my friends," Miguel said, bringing me back to reality. "Everyone is probably aware of the pictures of the Mayans and the Aztecs and the Toltec sacrificing bodies? Right here is where they did it."

"Oh, good Lord, don't tell me!," I thought.

"No," Miguel said, "We are not going to sacrifice your bodies and tear out your hearts. But what the Toltec people were taught by Jesus and by the Masters, is that just as Jesus' death healed so many people and actually healed so much out beyond in the universe, so too would their Spiritual deaths, or releases, help heal the people of earth and all that is out 'there.' The people who had not yet made the journey, who had no understanding of the process of men/women becoming God, only saw a physical body sacrificed ... which in reality, did not happen."

Later on our trip, Miguel further elaborated about sacrifices. At a certain time, known only by the Masters, a "cyclical/seasonal" point came where it was necessary for the Masters to ascend back to their origins. They primarily left because of what they believed was a shift between good and evil, and an "evil season" was about to happen. In retrospect, this was the coming of Cortez and the Spaniards. For some reason, the apprentices to the Masters did not know about the Masters' departures. So, not knowing the real truth behind the releasing, "sacrificing of" the Spiritual, double etherical bodies, what was meant to be a spiritual sacrifice became a physical one. Hence, you have the well known history of the Aztecs who tore out live, beating hearts, for a sacrifice to the Gods.

But knowing the real, spiritual truth behind the "sacrifices," Miguel told us that it was also on this spot, the precise center and top of the Pyramid of the Sun, that Jesus and other Masters would often leave to go back to where they were needed. It was our responsibility now, as people who had completed the journey, to release a part of ourselves to the universe or back to God, however you want to see transition, and to take our place as important healers of the world/universe.

I laid down on top of the center of the pyramid. I seemed to feel an energy from the Earth come up the center of the pyramid and go right through me and again take me out to the center of the universe. I felt an explosion within me and I became light which beamed its healing rays back to our planet Earth and all those upon it, and at the same time, out and beyond, wherever need be. It was an awesome feeling! A feeling I will never forget. To a degree, it is the same feeling I have experienced after receiving Holy Communion. I would then direct that communion out to one in the congregation who I knew was in need of healing ... a feeling of expandedness, purpose, a sharing in the role of Jesus. All because I believed it was happening at that moment. **"Whoever believes in me and the one who sent me, will do all that I have done and far greater"** (John 14:12). It is true! Step by step, day by day, we can take steps to heal ourselves and our world.

"It Is Finished"

To be in alignment with Jesus and the Father! What a way to end our journey at Teotihuacan. So much ground covered! How to put it all together? Let me try. Oftentimes when people are troubled, I tell them to think about the example of a Persian tapestry. On the back side of the rug, you see all the knots and frays, the miss-matches and the loose ends. But when you look at the tapestry from the top/ front (from God's view), you see a beautiful pattern being woven ... a Masterpiece! So it is when you look at the over- all picture of Teo. You see the hell which we all create and which is perpetuated by societies, religions, families and self. From an overall picture you see how an example has been set before us to get out of hell and get to heaven ... now. You see that in the end (and the beginning), it was God's plan for us to be created in God's image and to live as an image, an aspect of God. To do the things which Jesus did and far greater—to love, heal, forgive, understand and harmonize with the universe and its Creator. As Joseph Campbell says, "To live life in bliss, each moment."

And so it was, with that new enlightenment, we jour- neyed back into the city of smog and reality, snail-paced traffic and lots of mañanas. But this time, it was not so oppressive. The people looked different, or should I say, I felt different toward the people. They were all people who had the potential to get out of the hell which was around them. Even in the midst of a smoggy city, they could feel their true selves and realize who they were in relationship to God, the creator, father and mother.

God as mother. "God as woman," sure is a strange term or concept for many people. The last leg of our journey before the airport was a visit to the shrine of Our Lady of Guadalupe. Many of you may know the story so I will only retell it in an abbreviated form. The month was December in the year 1531. Juan Diego was a poor Indian peasant traveling across the hills at "Tepeyac" in what is now Mexico City. It was in the dead of winter and not much vegetation was growing. At one spot on the hill, as he took time to rest, the Blessed Mother Mary appeared before him. She told him to go tell the parish priest to build a church in her honor. Juan Diego, as an indigenous Indian, must have been familiar with the fact that the spot near which she

appeared was a place known to the Indians as the site of the
Aztec temple dedicated to "Tonantzin," the Earth Goddess,
associated with Mother-Earth energy. Maybe this appearance and request were not all that surprising for him. But
to tell a Catholic priest about this must have been a bit more
difficult. Well, as you can imagine, the priest thought he
was crazy. To make a beautifully long story short, Mary
appeared to him several other times and on the last time,
she told him to take the roses "over there" and put them in
his *tema* (apron) and deliver them to the priest. There were
no roses at this time of the year, but he turned around and
saw roses. He put them in his tema and headed off to the
priest. When he laid the flowers before the pastor, on the
face of the tema was the image, a full-body view, of what
is now the famous picture of Our Lady of Guadalupe. Since
then, a cathedral has been built near the spot and millions
of people have come to receive Mary's blessings.

We climbed up a short hill behind the actual cathedral to
a small chapel on top. Miguel had us all buy rosaries for
ourselves or for friends and then he told us that he was
going to bless them with the power of the Mother Mary
energy. A slight traditional twinge went through me thinking about whether he could bless or not ... but it left quickly.
After all, you bless your food at the meal, or you bless a
friend after they sneeze. His blessing would be just as
intense, especially with my own intent that these rosaries
would be blessed. Well, the rosaries were blessed in the
front of the sanctuary. Before I tell you what happened next
with Jesus, I would like to tell you about these rosaries. I
have always taken mine with me when I am doing healing
work, that is, anointing people with the holy oils in what is
called the sacrament of the sick. I have told each person that
these rosaries were specially blessed at the site where Mary
appeared to Juan Diego, and that they are to help in the
healing process. Each person, without an exception, has felt
a soothing, warm feeling when they held the rosary. Even
the kids in the high school, when I have used it for football

injury healings or a general energy-increasing healing, have felt a tingle go through their bodies. I personally thank the Blessed Mother's energy and love for this gift and pray you can experience the same.

After we had received the blessed rosaries, I took a moment to kneel before the altar at the sanctuary railing. I closed my eyes and in an instant, saw Jesus standing within the sanctuary. His hands were down and splayed out a little to the side with his palms facing forward. He was wearing only the same white garment he wore around his waist when he was crucified. BUT, he had three sacred hearts in his chest area. There was a large one on top, a medium-sized heart lower, and then a smaller one down toward the stomach. I was awestruck, almost too stunned to say anything. But of course, I had to ask why three hearts and what he doing there. "Patrick," he said, "I have come here in honor of my blessed mother and in honor of you."

"Why the three hearts?," I asked.

"These three hearts are to show you how much I love you. I have not just one but three hearts worth of love for you." I began to cry, as I do even now as I write this passage. More amazingly, he then went on to say, "And I want you to go back to your people and tell them that this is how much I love them also."

So that brought it all back home. Going to Teotihuacan to understand myself better, to find out more about God in my life, to take off the masks, to see the beautiful person I was ... where does it lead me? Right smack dab back to where I came from: enmeshed in the people, trying to be a reflection to them of how beautiful they, you, are as an important part of God and in God's world. The Alpha and the Omega. You, me, us and them from beginning to end ... a perfect, never-ending, circle of love.

NOTES

"Dedicated to The Ones I love"... Catholics!
and those stuck in similar organized religions!

What can **YOU** get out of this journey? Surely I don't
want you to pack your bags and get on the next plane to
Mexico City? And this is not *Close Encounters of the Third
Kind* where Richard Dreyfuss builds a mountain that he
constantly sees in his dreams, right in the middle of his
family's living room! I could just see it now: go out and get
10,000 bricks to start with and make the Avenue of the
Dead in your back yard ... *not*! No, no building, no airplane
trips. But what you *could* do is some journaling in a private
book just for you. You could do some theme meditations
weekly or daily, if that is your practice. But I think if you
go through the Teo process in some form or another, it can
be invaluable to your Spiritual growth and your understanding of yourself, your Spirit. Whether it be in writing,
contemplating or visualizing, take some time to look at the
following:

Leaving Hell:

Who or what are the judge and the jury in your life? List
the shoulds and the should nots in your life. See how you
can make all these secondary to your relationship of unconditional love with God. That love, that bonding, that foundation is the only thing that "should" matter in your life.
Say, when you go to bed, when you get up, with every
breath you breathe: "God loves me. I love myself as God
loves me. God and I are love." In your mediations or
visualizations, see these shoulds and should nots dissolve,
surrender into God's bright light. In your journal, list in one
column the "s" words or phrases, then counteract them on
the other side with the "God and Love" phrases.

Arena 1: Your Funeral

Go to a space in your back yard, your favorite place in nature, or even to your local parish church (if there would be sufficient private time and privacy). Find or bring a rock to represent your tombstone. Preside over your own funeral. This may require you to make a few notes before you come, so that you will know what to say for your eulogy. Praise yourself, bury the past with the past, let bad bygones be gone! Be your family and feel a sense of pride in all that God would see. If you can't find these good things for yourself, ask another, or better yet, sit quietly and listen to God. Make this space in time a reference point in the future for those days that seem to be all mucked up. Reposition yourself back to your grave and your new beginning when these times happen. Then go forth!

Creation of a Spiritual Self:

I think this exercise was particularly pertinent for the space of Teo because many belief systems there were attempting to (and did) accomplish many results. But let's look at it in a way that can be helpful to you today, where you are. What would it be like for you to see your Spirit in the form that it was originally created, how God sees you? If you can conceive how that would look or be, then maybe you need to see that more often. Look to see what you can attain, what you can learn from "It," Yourself. Take some quiet time and sit on your couch or out in your back yard and set a chair across from you for your other Self. Dialog with that Self.   Ask your Self, "What do you need?" "What can change?" "How can you love yourself more?" "How can you see God in yourself and others better?" The more we ask our Selves these learning and growing questions, the more we will become who we are. We will be able to say, "I Am." ... One last suggestion here. When you are finished with this dialog, see, believe, visualize the two of you getting up and embracing and merging together to become one. Then take a deep breath and move on in your day.

Arena 2:   Your Mind—Give Up the Fight!

Sometimes I used to (and sometimes I still do!) go to bed or get up in the morning and hear this ridiculous conversation going on in my mind. No, I'm not hearing voices in the crazy sense, but to the degree that I listen to these voices and allow them to rule my life, I am, to a degree, crazy. As I discussed in this part of the journey of Teo, "Who's in control here?" All I can suggest you do for this part is to actually speak out loud, if speaking silently to yourself doesn't work as well, and say: "Hey, I give up here! I will no longer have this conversation with you! No more battling back and forth! Yeah, sure, you can win, but I ain't buying into it anymore!" Next time you hear another "should" or "shouldn't," say or remember and reiterate that you trust yourself enough to live life in the best, proper, loving, divine way that you can. You are protected, you are guided, you are growing, you are going forth. You have no need to struggle along the way with the mind. In psychology, there is a technique which is called mind stopping. You put a rubber band around your wrist. Every time you have one of these thoughts or conversations come up, you snap the rubber band and you end the conversation. Teo says you can accomplish this result much quicker when you create a belief system that says you are no longer a part of the game. See it, pray it, live it, believe it, exercise it in your heart and your life will become a soothing symphony without all the dissonant sounds.

Arena 3: Healing the Memories

There are so many marvelous programs today that deal with healing the memories. The Fifth Step of the Twelve Steps of Alcoholics Anonymous asks to makes amends for all the hurt that has been done in the past and make every effort to right it. The Ling brothers are two famous Catholic priests who have promoted a program in the charismatic movement called "Healing of the Memories." All these tech= niques are provided for us to realize the need to let go of the past ... especially around sexual issues. These issues seem to be the velcro that sticks most to the lining of the mind.

We, in the Catholic church, have an excellent way to move through past issues. That way is called the Sacrament of Reconciliation. We don't call it confession anymore be- cause the emphasis is not on reiterating that we have been bad, bad, bad! We don't call it penance anymore because our love from God does not depend on what we have to do to make it up to get back God's love. Remember the Prodi- gal Son story? The father didn't say you have to work it off before you can come into my house! The sacrament (mean- ing "God is present") is called reconciliation because we want to acknowledge the fact that God is with us, eyeball to eyeball, as the word reconcile means. SO, I encourage you to find a priest with whom you can feel very comfortable. Do a little research here and ask around to discover a com- panion on the path of enlightenment. (And if for some unfortunate reason, you cannot find a priest to give you some sacred time, then take time with your best friend who loves you unconditionally.) Then, after doing some exami- nation of conscience to see what is sticking to the walls of your mind, make an appointment for a good deal of time and sit down with the priest, believing in the same sense of the Toltecs about the magicalness of the rock as a sacred spot in the second arena. Create a time for a healing of your memories of the past. AND, equally important, receive the blessing from the priest or your best friend and know that this is strengthening you to reevaluate your beliefs on what makes you bad or good in the eyes of God. Sense a feeling of liberation as you leave this reconciliation experience. Even take a moment to celebrate this new freedom. Buy something new for yourself. Take a walk on the beach. Watch a sunset. Hold a baby.

See yourself not as a bad child doomed to repeat "crimes of the past," so to speak, but see yourself as a prodigal son or daughter who has come into this world to celebrate life ... to live and learn, to fall and get up ... to walk with the Creator, God, the forever loving Father.

Arena 4: Fire

I am going to ask you to allow your buttons to be pushed just a little bit more. This arena asked you to recollect that you may have been here before and that it is necessary to walk in another's shoes so that you can be more loving of all. Barriers and walls block us from experiencing the fullness of life. We create those barriers and we and God can dissolve those same barriers.

There are two things you can do. First of all, I ask you again to openly examine your conscience. Bring forth all those people who rub you wrong. This can be done individually, but it may be better to look at this exercise collectively. Who are "they" that you consider your enemy? Those of different color ... nationality ... sexual orientation ... those less economically fortunate than you ... political agenda different? Take a day off from work, or maybe even two days, and find a way that you can spend some time to work with, rub elbows with, those you find difficult. Work in a homeless shelter; an orphanage in the barrio or a single mothers' day-care center; a convalescent home for the particular nationality that you begrudge; help serve meals for AIDS patients; find someone who belongs to a political party other than yours and attend a meeting; go with this group when they do some charity work with the least of Jesus' brother and sister; at Christmas time, quietly take 100 $1-bills and distribute them on the corners to the poorest of the poor who can't even thank you ... and there is no way to wiggle out of this! If you are reading this and you are

Catholic, your parish has every resource information possible to find an agency where you can take the opportunity to walk in another's shoes.

To accomplish the same task a different way, we return to that sacred moment of holy communion during Mass. I know many people do not pay attention to what they received, especially right after receiving for communion. I see them going through their purses, talking with their neighbors and even shaking hands with the people coming up to receive communion. No guilt ... just a suggestion of how to better spend your time. When you see a person go up for communion that looks different from you or maybe, God forbid, you judge them unworthy, remember the same God that is giving them communion gave you the same bread of life. God does not discriminate, why should you? Every scantily dressed teenager, every traditional person who kneels down for communion, every Black, Asian, Mexican, Anglo, Filipino, is seen as the same in the eyes of God . Re-collect all of you into one family of God and stop building barriers. Begin holding hands, either literally or Spiritually, to help build the Kingdom of God on earth. I guarantee it, you will feel stronger and healthier and wiser for this rebuilding action.

Heaven: An Altar for God

When I stood before the portal in "heaven" I felt as though, no, I KNEW that Jesus was coming right through that energy spot to speak and be with me. I once was engaged in a shamanic inner-journey meditation during which I went underground to a room filled with golden treasures as far as the eye could see. In the middle of this room was a spiral staircase leading up to the ceiling. I took the stairs up and when I opened the trap door, it came right out into the altar in the middle of my church. The message I was getting was that the Catholic church was filled with so many treasures and we need to take greater advantage of them.

SO, the first thing you can do is focus in on the altar at church, be it during quiet time or if possible, during Mass. Allow Jesus to come off the cross (usually behind the altar) and come down to the altar to share with you his wisdoms and insights for your life. Allow this sacred spot to be the place where God speaks to you, in silence. Or listen to God through *some* of the words of the priest. Be nourished through the creation of a sacred substance we believe is the body and blood of Christ. Absorb God through the readings of the sacred scripture, or even through the harmonies or the words of the sacred music being played nearby. Create, allow and receive. **The Source** is right there before you. *Use* it for your highest potential and good.

I would also encourage you to find or create some sacred space in your home. If you can create this space, it will reflect within your life that you are special and sacred. For in reality, you are a sacred altar for God. God reveres you with the same power you do God. Put around this altar in your home your sacred articles and symbols from your religion. Bring to your altar your sacred stones or shells you have collected from Mother Earth as a sign of creation; put a candle to reflect your light and love; place the sacred feathers or carvings from the animal world; present flowers from the plant world to represent God's love for creation. Then, when you have a prayer or a petition or desire to meditate for clarification or wisdom, and cannot make it to church, come before your altar of God. There, too, you shall receive the Master Jesus and your guardian angels to assist you in your growth.

Pyramid of the Sun/Son:

"I felt an explosion within me and I became light which beamed its healing rays back to our planet earth and all

those upon it and at the same time, out and beyond, wherever need be. It was an awesome feeling! One I will never forget."

That was the feeling I had on top of the Pyramid of the Sun. Have you ever felt that after you received communion from the Son? I want to empower you to know that you can have the same feeling, the same effect. Just turn off the wandering mind, the wandering eyes, and focus your attention, like a laser beam of light, FROM the center of your being (where this, just-received Holy Communion went to). Focus this Light of the World to any part of your body that needs healing; to any part of another person's body that needs healing; send it to surround your church so that all who enter may do so in a Spirit of peace and receptivity of God's love. Send this bread of life, through the power of your unlimited mind, to envelop and feed the entire world with peace and harmony and love. Just allow your Self to do that four Sundays a month and I am sure you will see a change in your life and those around you. You will be empowered, as Jesus wanted us to be, to do all the things he did and far greater. Awesome! Radical! Just as Jesus.

Our Lady of Guadalupe: Our Mother

Again, I am not asking you to jump on the plane and experience the energy of the exact spot upon which Mary visited Juan Diego. Nor am I asking you to start saying the rosary all day long. But I am asking you to see that which is really all around you.

Just the other day, I was reading an introduction to a new book, *Through Time into Healing,* by Brain Weiss, M.D. The introduction was written by Raymond Moody, M.D. He was the famous doctor who wrote the series *Life after Death* about the near-death experiences [NDE] of many thousands of people who had been declared clinically dead, and then "brought back from the dead." They described beautiful encounters with God, Jesus, Mary, Buddha, or other Masters. Once back, their lives were changed for the better. In this introduction, Moody describes a new method which he believes will become prevalent in a few years, a method which he has experienced himself. He has uncovered a process which allows you to talk directly to someone who has died. You would be talking with them just as if they were sitting in a chair before you. Interesting that a medical doctor would be discussing this practice and not some theologian. Now, I'm not sure whether this is going to come about or not ... but what an impact this would have on a person's life! ... if you were able to talk to a loved one that had died and passed on to the Spirit world.

I believe that as we get in contact with Mary, let alone Jesus, in the same way, then our lives, too, will be changed dramatically. Use any method possible to achieve this relationship, this dialog. I have asked so many people in confession, in counselling, in friendships, to come to believe that the blessed Mother is wrapping her gentle arms around them as only a mother would do. I asked that they place their trust in her in the guidance of their lives; that they trust her healing power just as a mother magically kisses her child who has injured itself. Place a favorite rosary on your altar at home and know that it is being energized for healing all you pray for or with. Or, ask the priest to bless it and then use it with the full knowledge of its power.

Finally, place a picture of Mary (the one from Medjegore is especially beautiful as well as the one from Our Lady of Guadalupe) and a picture of Jesus on your altar. Just as Jesus told me to tell all of you that he has (at least) three sacred hearts full of love for you, hear Mary and Jesus tell you daily how much they love you and your Spirit. Hear this! Hear this! Hear this enough until you are able to love unconditionally your own Spirit and soul.

Following any of these suggestions will have the same impact upon you as the Toltec Masters, Jesus and God, had for the world over the ages. God did not intend divine inspiration to begin and then stop at the life and death of Jesus. The church has always believed that the Holy Spirit is alive and growing and opening new windows, new horizons, new ways to see our Creator. As you continue to deepen your understanding of God and Jesus in your life, your journey as a Spiritual being in search of human experiences shall become a grand adventure filled with blessings, Beauty and wonderment. I would like to end this chapter with a poem I have used in Mass and the classroom. May it help you appreciate your journey in this present moment of eternity:

> *I was regretting the past*
> *and fearing the future.*
> *Suddenly God was speaking:*
> ***"My name is I AM"***
> *He paused ... I waited.*
>
> *He continued,*
> *"When you live in the past,*
> *with its mistakes and regrets,*
> *It is hard. I am not there.*
> *My name is not I WAS"*
>
> *"When you live in the future,*
> *with its problems and fears,*
> *It is hard. I am not there.*
> *My name is not I WILL BE."*
>
> *"When you live in this moment*
> *It is* **not** *hard. I am here.*
> ***My name is I AM."***

Peace and love be with you all NOW on your journey through life and light.

Sunday Sermons

This is a sermon/homily I gave during Lent a few weeks before Holy Week and Easter. The Gospel dealt with Jesus going into the desert and being tempted by the Devil. This is a great homily to insert at the end of this chapter, particularly in light of the section dealing with hell and sin.

Today's message of sin and temptation is a very difficult subject to talk about. It makes people (us) feel uncomfortable. But because it is Lent, we need to examine more closely our relationship with God and Jesus and see what makes it work and what doesn't. Sin (turning away from God), and temptation (being distracted from God) are two aspects which hinder our relationship.

There are two ways we can approach sin and temptation. I would like to tell you a story to show you these ways. First of all, there once was a small child in church who was turning around and smiling at everyone. He wasn't gurgling, spitting, making noise, or tearing the song books or even making a mess of his mother's handbag. He was just smiling at everyone: **a big smile from ear to ear**. But then suddenly his mother jerked him around, and in a stage whisper that everyone could hear, she said: "Stop grinning ... you are in church!" Now with that, she gave him a belt on his hindside and as the tears rolled down his cheeks, she added, "Now that's better!" She returned to her prayers. That mother really made the kid's life miserable. And when we are talking about sin and temptation, we (the church or the priest) can really make life miserable for you. We can point the finger and say, "Bad boy!" or "Bad girl!" and make tears roll down your face, and make you feel uncomfortable. You can even make yourself feel bad when you think about sin and temptation. We, as priests, don't even need to stand up here and do the bad deed. You can do that yourself!

But, I think there is another way to deal with sin and temptation. Many have taught that sin is a violation of a moral code. Now as true as that may be, there is an easier way to put it: in truth, sin is only error. You can act in a way that is against your divine nature. And your divine nature is to love God, yourself and others. That is an act of commission. **Or,** you don't act in a way that is your divine nature. That is a sin of omission because you don't follow your true desires to follow the words of Christ. When you act in either of these ways, commission or omission of a sin, you do it out of ignorance of your true identity. You forget who you are.

But God doesn't stop loving you and God doesn't want you to get stuck in all the guilt and bad feelings. God wants you to learn and change. And if you don't believe that, then reread the story of the Prodigal Son. That son (or daughter), out of ignorance, left the father and then, because of a realization of his true identity, came back to a father who laid no guilt trips on him. The father only said, "I love you and I want us to celebrate life."

When the devil came to tempt Jesus, Jesus had no problem dealing with him because he had his eyes on

God and knew that God was his source of life. Like the baby in the opening story, Jesus concentrated on life and happiness, not on the negative or empty promises which came from the devil.

We have to realize that God is the center of our lives, and then we have to live and love life. When we have this attitude we won't be tempted to give in to the temptation of sin. Jesus said, "Know this truth and the truth will set you free."

We need to know that Lent is not a time of gloom and doom but a time of vital growth, a true springtime of the soul. Life is always springtime if we allow ourselves to smile and focus on God. It is springtime when we don't play guilt trips on ourselves for making an error or giving in to temptation. We arise from faulty situations and get back on our feet and on the right path.

Like the little kid knew in the opening story: Life is one big smile from ear to ear if you allow it to be. *Amen!*

This sermon/homily was on love. This is an excellent homily to place after the last one on sin and temptation. In the process you go through in Teo (the pyramids outside of Mexico), you must first realize the sins and temptations you have created in your life. Then you have to realize that, in order to move out of that "arena," you have to move into love.

On a moonlit night in the Garden of Eden, Adam asked Eve, "Do you love me?" Eve replied, "Yes, of course—who else?"

Morning, noon, and night, we may ask Jesus the same question, "Jesus, do you love me?" And day after day we always get the same reply: "Who else?"

And so we hear the same message in the Gospel today in several spots: First, Jesus said, "I will ask the Father and he will give you another when I go, to be with you always." And secondly, Jesus says, "I will not leave you an orphan; I will come back for you." AND, "On that day when I come back for you, you will know that I am in my Father and you are in me and I am in you." All of us together, ourselves, Jesus and God. Now if that doesn't show us that Jesus loves us, I don't know what will. Finally, in today's Gospel, Jesus says all this love he had for us is based on the fact that we love Jesus. Wow, what an easy task!

It seems so simple: We have to love Jesus. Not too hard to do considering the fact that he dies for us; that he will never leave us alone even if we can't tell he is there, that he has guaranteed you and me a place in heaven ("In my Father's house there are many mansions").

All that makes it pretty easy to love Jesus. As it said in the reading, "Venerate the Lord, that is Christ, in your hearts." So we love him and then his love doubles back to us. But, is it so easy to be loved by Jesus?

There once was a loving wife who was trying to do little things to perk up her husbands' sagging Spirit. One day she decided to replace his stuffy conservative wardrobe with more colorful and youthful-looking clothes. "It might be good for his self image," she thought. So she ventured into the men's clothing section of the department store, and said to the sales woman, "I'm looking for something wild and exciting in slacks." And the saleswoman replied, "Aren't we all, my dear, aren't we all!"

I think it is a human trait that we are always looking for something that will make our lives better. But the problem is that when our dream seems to come true (whether it is a new house, car, or better job, or even something wild and exciting in slacks), the realization of it somehow never quite lives up to the expectation. We seem to be constantly building ourselves up for a big letdown. Maybe the fact that we just say we love Jesus isn't the secret that makes our life complete, and therefore entitled to receive God's love. If we look to the gospel, we see that Jesus did say something more. He says, "If you love me *and* obey the commands I give you." Ah ha! What are the commands that he gave us?

Love God, we all seem to do that. Love others; hmmm, a bit harder. Love ourselves; maybe just as hard as loving another.

So, in order to feel God's love more in our lives, it looks like we have a little bit of homework ahead in our lives. We need to start loving everyone [and everything] around us. Try it. Think of someone you have real difficulty loving or liking and just say, "For God's sake, I love _____," and fill in the blank. Take a moment to do that. No qualifications, no ifs, ands, or buts. Just say, "I love _____," and let God do the rest.

And work on loving yourself! If there is something you don't like about yourself, or something you think God doesn't like about you (not!), say, "I love myself just as God loves me." Let's say that one out loud. *"I love myself, just as God loves me!"* By saying these two statements, you are allowing God to return that love back to you.

So practice that love and receive a little love of yourself from God. That is what the gospel, the good news, is all about.

And s-o-o-o on a moonlit night in the Garden of Eden, God asked us, "Do you love me?" And not only did we say, "Yes, who else," but also, "Yes; how else but by loving others and ourselves." *Amen!*

Chapter Five
Psychic Surgery
"The Hand of God"

*"Come on Father! You can't be
that naive to think that he is
actually putting his hand into
someone's body without first
cutting it with a knife! He's
got to be using chicken blood or
optical illusions!"*

f you remember back to the introduction material,
you will recall my encounter with a Mexican
Curandera (healer) named Sarita. She was the
first person to open up my mind to the fact that there were
other alternatives to bodywork aside from the traditional
medical field. As I watched her work on cancer patients, I
would see her move her hands over the body as if she was
opening it up with scalpels. But there was no intrusion of
the body. No blood and guts, so to speak. After making
this imaginary opening, she made movements similar to
removing "bad" material and discarding "it" to the ground.
Then with one hand raised to the heavens, she would, with
the other hand, point her index finger into the imaginary
opening or affected area then "inject" what she called God's

medicine. Once that was finished, she would move her fingers over the area as if she were putting in stitches. The most important statement that I constantly heard Sarita say after each operation is that it was God that was doing the healing, not her.

I suppose if I were well versed in the laying on of hands, a method used in the Catholic church by priests, deacons and healers, I would think that this form of healing by Sarita is simply just one step removed; a few more different, unique motions. During the Anointing of the Sick ceremony, the priest is asked to pause and lay his hands over the person, often times, lightly over the head. The priest would call upon the Holy Spirit to pour forth its divine presence. So many, many times we were ministering to seriously ill people in the hospital. Although I haven't taken a poll, I would say that most priests were not "betting" on a miracle to happen. Usually, the anointing was to put the person mentally and spiritually at ease, and remind them that they were in God's hands. Regardless of the outcome of their illness, they would be with God. With non-deathbed illnesses, through continued prayer and the will of God, hope was held that a person could always recover, despite the odds. Now there are a few priests, and we are talking about a very small percentage compared to the total number of priests, who believe in faith healings, especially in serious cases. Through the power of prayer and the laying on of hands, they have witnessed miraculous healings.

Another, relatively new liturgy (service) for Catholics is the Anointing of the Sick communal service. This was held as a community event, either within a Sunday liturgy or at a different, special time. At these services, the parishioners were encouraged to join in prayer for their sick sisters and brothers. At a specific time during the liturgy, those in need of healing were called forward and anointed by the priests. Although I thought these services were a step in the right direction, two things "bothered" me. First of all, I always remembered one of my pastors stressing to the people that these anointings were only for those in need of physical healings. "Don't come up if you're having a bad day, a fight with your spouse, or mental stress." Whatever *that* meant! Hmmm, I thought healing was healing. I always left out that part when I officiated at the service. In a round about way, I'd encourage anyone in need of healing to come up. The lines always seemed longer at the services over which I presided.

Secondly, only the priest was to do the laying on of hands. That denies the fact which I present in this chapter, that it is everyone's divine right to participate in healing. I remember at one AIDS healing Mass I presided over. I bypassed this exclusion. I asked everyone, at the direction-leadership of the priest (me), to come forth and lay hands on those in need. If they could not directly touch the person due to the size of the crowd, then come forth and extend their hand and send light, love and healing power.

With that in mind,, I knew Sarita's unorthodox method of healing would not be looked favorably upon by the church as equal to the priest's role. BUT ... being the open Spirit that I was, I placed it in a file back in the brain and knew that some more goodness about this· experience would come forth somewhere down the pike.

Ten years later, I received a call from Jacque telling me about a most unusual phenomenon she had just experienced. As I have mentioned before she explores new horizons and integrates new findings into her life with determination. So I knew when she told me about the renowned psychic surgeon, Alex Orbito, I was going to participate in another leap in faith.

Before I explain the details about Alex, I would first like to lay some foundations about psychic surgery. Psychic surgery is the ability to physically enter the body without any instrumentation. Here's how I explained it to the kids in my senior World Religion class in high school, before showing them a video of the actual healing procedures of Alex. I start with a water molecule. Something everyone knows about ... simple old H_2O. I draw the two hydrogen atoms and one oxygen atom on the board in a real close configuration. Then I say, "If we magnified that 100 times, we would see that there is 'space' among the three atoms. What is that space?" I then tilt the microscope, so to speak, and ask them to imagine looking out a telescope. Envision how huge this universe is. Think of the distance between the nearest planet, star, or galaxy. Once a person gave me the following facts, "There are at least four **billion** suns in the Milky Way which is in **one** galaxy." (WOW! That just blows my mind!) The facts continued:

> ... Many of these suns are thousands of times larger than our own, and vast millions of them have whole planetary systems, including billions of satellites. And all of this revolves at the rate of about a million miles an hour, like a huge oval pinwheel. Our own sun and its planets, which includes the earth, are on the edge of this wheel. This is only our own small corner of the universe, so why do not these billions of revolving and rotating suns and planets collide? The answer is, the space is so unbelievably vast that if we reduced the suns and planets in correct mathematical proportion with relation to the distances between them, each sun would be a speck of dust, two, three, and four thousand miles away from its nearest neighbor. And, mind you, that is only the Milky Way—our own small corner—our own galaxy. How many galaxies are there? Billions. Billions of galaxies spaced at about one million light years apart (one light year is about six trillion miles). Within the range of our biggest telescopes, there are at least one hundred million separate galaxies such as our own Milky Way, and that's not all, by any means. The scientists have found that the further you go out into space with telescopes, the thicker the galaxies become, and there are billions and billions still uncovered by the scientist's camera and the astrophysicist's calculations.

What is all the space that holds that massive mixture together? Go back to the smaller scale of H_2O. "It's my belief," I tell the students, "that this space is God. And when we realize that everything is not as solid as we think it is, but is filled with God-space, then we can break or dissolve our old concepts of solidness. We can pierce new planes, new walls, new bodies!" At least some of the kids stare at me with that look on their face that says, "What is he talking about?"

So I ask them this question, "Do you know anybody who can walk through walls?"

"No way!," come the shouts.

Then after a little prodding and reminding that this is a religious school, so think religion, I ask the question again. "Do we know of anyone in our faith history who appeared in a room that was locked?"

"Oh yeah, Jesus!"

The Bible clearly states in the Gospel of Luke, chapter 24, verse 36 and on, that Jesus appeared to the twelve apostles after he had been crucified. They tell us that the door was locked. We know he didn't enter through the usual means. We are also told (Luke 24:42–43) that he ate with his friends. Therefore, we know he had some semblance of a physical body. "Look at my hands and my feet, see that it is I myself. Feel me, you will know, for a ghost doesn't have flesh and bones, as you can see I have." (Luke 24:39–40). He did this several times for we have the accounts with and without Thomas being present (John 20:19–23 and then in John 20:24–29). Thomas held the same belief as many of my students. Surely his friend couldn't have walked through a locked door, let alone, be alive after having suffered an excruciating death on the cross. But Thomas *saw* and he believed. How did he believe? He probed the hands of Jesus where the nail marks had been and he placed his hand within Jesus's side where the lance had thrust an opening. So Thomas believed that Jesus was alive, and alive in a new form which seemed to have broken all the concepts of solid material. This Jesus walked through walls, ate solid food and yet was Spirit. It is again my belief, based on *what I have seen,* that Jesus came to understand that the material, physical plane was not solid. In the days of old, if a person were to be healed without medical procedures, it would be considered a miracle. Now, what we would consider miracles in the past can be performed for all with a Christ understanding!

When I first met Alex Orbito, he looked as though he was a doctor who had just performed ten major surgeries in ten hours. I later found out that this little Filipino man had just returned from a trip to Germany and Sweden and was now back to the United States to help the people of Southern California. I was wrong about him doing ten operations in ten hours. He had performed hundreds of surgeries in a couple of days! Although he looked tired, he was revitalized when he saw almost one hundred new smiling faces anxious, yet ready to be a part of his healing. (See picture of Jacqueline Snyder, Alex Orbito and me on page 136.)

Alex told us about his own personal history. In a nutshell, his healing ministry began when he was fourteen. An old woman in his village who had been paralyzed for over ten years had a dream that she was to ask Alex, this little fourteen year old boy, to come heal her. He came to her as he was told. When he laid his hands on her, he felt like Alex Orbito wasn't there any more. It was as if an energy force from God went through him and into this old woman. After ten minutes, she started to move her fingers and toes. Twenty minutes passed and she could move parts of her paralyzed body. In 30 minutes, she was able to get up and walk around. His reputation spread like wildfire! He started doing a hundred healings in a day, getting paid only one chicken egg for every healing. It wasn't until five years later that during one operation, he actually, after laying his hands on a person, broke the plane of the body and his hands slipped in. Once inside, they seemed to act like a magnet and attracted a sizable piece of tissue which he calls negative matter. Then he pulled his hand out, said a prayer over the area and the incision disappeared! He later explained that he sees the body like water. After all, he tells us, scientists say the body is 80 percent water. When he removes his hand from the body, it closes up just like removing your hand from water. You can't tell where it has been. As I was listening to him give his talk, I sat there

Jacqueline Snyder, Alex Orbito
& Author.

probably not unlike Thomas and thought, "I want to see this!"

Before telling what I saw (and more!), I need to tell you one other aspect which I think you will find interesting. Alex is totally Christian! When I first heard him give his talk, he was saying in a very forceful tone that the way for the salvation of the soul was through Jesus Christ! Jacque and I gave each other the eye, knowing that many of the people at this gathering had moved beyond a limited concept of "salvation." In flushing his theory out at a later time, I realized that Alex is aware that salvation means many things. He feels it mainly means that you come to love yourself, as Jesus taught. Why not? You are created from and by God. He says, "You should get up every morning and love every bit, every part of yourself. This love, this freedom to be yourself, is your salvation."

With regards to his healings gifts, he is in alignment with *The Christ.* Because of the guidance and love that Jesus shows him, and he in turn shares with others, Alex is able to raise his consciousness and understanding above some of the old concepts of the body, and perform these extraordinary healings. It is important to know also that Alex meditates every day. When he meditates, he focuses his concentration on God. Concentrating on God, he brings the light into his being, hands and heart, and purifies his thoughts and aligns his action with God, with love. When he does this, when he concentrates on the light, he does miraculous things.

Seeing (and experiencing) is BELIEVING!

Alex, like Sarita, realizes he is a channel of **God's** healing energy. Therefore, in reality, he doesn't need any client to come in and tell him specifically what needs to be healed. One could just come in, lie down before Alex, and God would direct him where to work. But, knowing full well humanity's anxieties of new experiences, Alex follows a procedure that helps alleviate worries and concerns. It also helps in cutting down the discovery time, as there are sometimes a hundred people waiting. Before seeing Alex, you write on a piece of paper three areas you would like him to work on. These can all be physical but are not limited to just that. Mental, emotional and spiritual levels are also healed through his work.

Now picture this: Jacque had already told me that Alex would be greatly honored to not only work on a Catholic priest, but also to have one (that's me) dressed in my black clerical clothes, present at his talks. He also asked that I say a prayer over the people before they entered the healing room. Okay! To get to the point of "seeing is believing," I will do almost (I said *almost*!) anything. I knew being in my collar would get me more "How do you do it, Father?" questions, but I was willing to open myself up to that so as to get to the heart of the experience. (No pun intended ... well, on second thought, why not keep it light?) Anyway, I was praying over people, with people, before they went into the healing room. I prayed that this experience would meet their deepest desires for perfect health, and that Alex could be used as an instrument of God's desire to have all people healed. Being healed, they would experience their fullness as sons and daughters of God. I would call upon Jesus and the Blessed Mother Mary and visualize them present, wrapping their loving arms around each person before me. Once, when I was in the middle of praying for one of the clients, Jacque came out of the room and said that Alex was ready to give a demonstration. Alleluia! Thank you, Jesus ... finally a chance to see!

The healing room was in the den of the host family. There had been a massage table set up and clean sheets had been placed over the table. When we entered, a woman, who had previously agreed with Alex that it would be all right to "use" her for a demonstration, was lying on the table and her belly was exposed. She had been diagnosed with cancer and the doctors were not very hopeful. When "Father" entered the room, I was allowed to move right up to the front to get a good view. I watched Alex like a hawk to see that he didn't have anything up his sleeve. Well, he didn't. In fact, he had his sleeves rolled up. Next I watched his hands. He explained to us that after praying and directing God's energy to the affected area, his left hand went down on the body first to act as an anesthetic. Then he placed his right hand down and "miraculously" his finger would pop through the plane, into the skin and a slit would appear. Then his finger, followed by a good part of his hand, would enter through the plane of the body. Several people in the room were quietly oohing and aahing. A few were getting a bit squeamish because there was blood oozing around the opening. You could hear a squeezy, sloshy sound. Soon he removed his hand, and a dark piece of substance about the size of a two-inch cube came out. He showed it and threw it away. (Once I saw him react like it had a negative charge to it and he threw it quickly into the garbage.) Finally, after removing several objects, he slowly took away his hands and there was no more incision, just the blood to wipe up. He then laid his hands over the area again to say a final healing prayer.

When we thought he was through with this particular lady, he told us not to leave because she still needed some overnight healing to remove toxins that had accumulated in her stomach due to the cancer. So he took a six-inch-long piece of cotton and poked it in another slit in her stomach. He told us that would stay there overnight and remove the toxins. In the morning he would remove it. I happened to be there the next morning and much to my surprise, he opened her up once more and delicately pulled out this long piece of cotton which had deteriorated to some extent. There were many black globs on the cotton. It reminded me of little black leeches. These were the toxins. During both of these surgeries, we asked the woman how she was feeling. She said it felt wonderful, almost like someone was tickling her inside. Remember there was no anesthesia, no suturing, no stitches and she was able to get right up off the table after this three- to five-minute procedure. After each surgery, she, as well as every one else who was worked upon, went to a room where they could recover. They rested, drank some water, were prayed with and soothed with calm, quiet music.

Okay, now I saw it! ... and I have watched the video tape of this surgery and others over and over to make sure it was "legit." Now what was I going to do? Did I now believe? If anyone knows the little boy in me as well as I am getting to know him, then my first thought was, "Let me get on that table and experience it!" I didn't have any physical thing wrong with me, but knew I could use a healing or cleansing or boost on the emotional or spiritual level. So I signed up to go in. I wrote down on my piece of paper that if there were any emotional trauma blockages from the past that had physically manifested in my body, then please remove them. I also asked that my "third eye," the chakra area which would help me see situations from a clear Spiritual perspective, be opened up too! So into the room and up on the table I went.

After I opened my shirt, Alex went right to an area below my sternum, in the middle of my rib cage. I asked him why he was starting there for my particular request. He said that area was one of my Spiritual areas. I felt a push into my body and the next thing I knew there was blood all over. He began pulling out a piece of "dark stuff." He doesn't talk much during the surgery as he is in a deep communion, trance-like state with God. So I didn't feel as though I could ask him to define where that piece came from or what or why. (See actual pictures of surgery on me on page 141.) He then went for my heart area and pulled something else out. I presume it was something that blocked my love of self, others and God from being complete. Finally, I felt him dig very hard into my forehead and he said, "Ah Father, you have a very bright third eye!" Within just a few

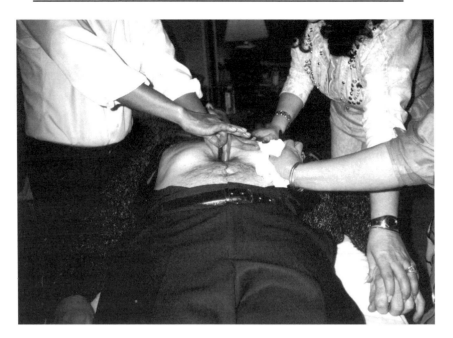

Author's Surgery

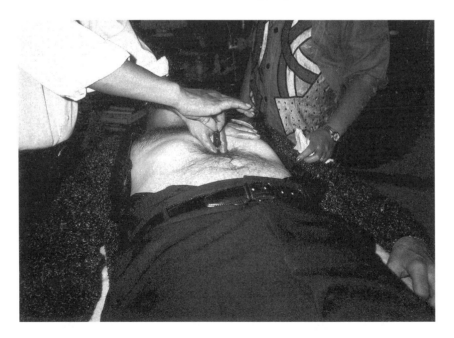

minutes the surgery was completed. The blood was wiped off. He said an inaudible prayer over my body as he laid his hands over me once more. Then he said, "Okay, Father," and I was ushered off into the living room to lie down and integrate what had just happened.

What had just happened? After looking back at the pictures and the video, I know that Alex had his hand in me. I knew that he had no chicken blood hidden anywhere, or anything that looked like a little dark piece of tissue hidden between his fingers. Although I more or less believed before the surgery, I now had the same *feeling*, the same sureness, that Thomas must have felt after he put his hands in Jesus' side. I saw and felt and believed without a doubt that the body is fluid and that the Christ is alive on many levels, on all levels.

Can You Believe It?

I know parts of this, maybe all of this, is hard to believe. Alex explains this dilemma in an enlightening way: We are trying to make $1 + 1 = 2$ and, in this area of psychic surgery, it can't. When it comes to dealing with God, $1 + 1 = 1$. We are all one with God and can relate, integrate, blend and enter into and with God on many different levels, yet they/ we are all the same One. Be open to God's wondrous, new, creative forces in your life. Release old, stagnant, dusty perspectives and be willing to explore new horizons.

As I write this chapter, I have just returned from another weekend of experiencing Alex's healing. Again, I assisted in praying over and for the people as they entered the healing room. I was touched at how readily people accepted me in my priestly collar. So often this weekend someone came up afterward and said that their mind was put to rest when they saw me there. There is so much good that can come from the Catholic church ... so much love and support for people who are taking the risk to explore new avenues for their journey. BUT ... at the general meeting where Alex spoke to a room filled with people about his history, another side of the church reared its head. I had given the introductions for Jacque and Alex, while also winding in a few fibers of my own story and how I came to be there. A woman came up to me after the meeting and I wasn't sure how to react, as she seemed to have fire in her eyes. She railed about how the church had damaged her with a fear-filled perspective of God. She often times felt that she was bad and guilt-ridden. With such an outlook on God and therefore life, she believed that she had passed this on to her children in the way she had raised them. This resulted in the need for many, many hours of therapy to untangle the unhealthy web she wove. Of course, I think a lot of other factors went into her stance and position in life, not just how the church had molded her. But her point after all this railing and wailing was: "Father, what a miracle it is to see you here with your collar and blacks on, telling us that it is okay to explore and to expand." Through many combinations: Alex, Jacque, myself and others, this woman was beginning to experience the salvation of her soul. She was beginning to feel good about herself and love life.

Psychic surgery doesn't have to just deal with a hand entering the plane of the body without medical instrumentation or procedures. Healing the body, healing our psyche, our soul, can be available to you through many means. Alex says to concentrate on God in yourself. That is healing. Alex entering the body is healing. Laying hands on a friend in pain or in need is a healing act. Being present to another in a nonjudgmental way (as I was to the lady after the meeting) is healing and realigns your soul to the truth that it is. People, explore as many new ways of receiving healing and giving others health on as many levels as you can. Jesus' life centered around realigning, healing others and "opening them up" to the truth of their relationship with the Creator. Experience this in your own lives today. All of this is re-discovering God, re-creating the Beauty that you are. **It is your right.**

What is my right? As I explained at the beginning of this chapter, we, as priests, are called on many times to administer the anointing of the sick. It's no longer called the "Last Rites" as so many refer to it. The anointing of the sick is scripturally based. The Letter of James, Chapter 5, from verse 13 on says, "Is anyone among you in trouble? He should pray. Is anyone happy? He should sing praises. Is there anyone who is sick? He should call forth the elders of the church who will pray for him and rub oil on him in the name of the Lord. This prayer made in faith, will heal the sick man; the Lord will restore him to health." As a priest, I have gained much confidence over the years to go out and anoint the sick with the understanding that they will get better. I have come to believe that the oil we use to bless the sick is holy and does help in creating a conduit for God's healing power. The stories are numerous.

In my first year as a priest, I remember going to visit a woman named Connie who was in the hospital with cancer of the nose. She is positive (and I later came to accept) that I was an instrument for the Lord's healing power. She is alive, well and "kicking" fifteen years later. In my many years as a priest, I have laid my hands on umpteen parishioners who have felt heat from my hands, who have felt that a Spiritual presence was present. Paul, although he died from brain cancer shortly after my visit, distinctly told me that he knew that a man and woman in Spirit were right by him when we started the healing prayers. Many people have recovered quicker than doctors have anticipated. Rich, who is a nonCatholic, but a husband of a devoted Catholic parishioner, has been close to death many times. When I came to pray with him and anoint him with the holy oil, I called upon Mary, Jesus and all my guardian angels and Master Teachers to be there to help me be a channel of God's healing power. Time after time, his wife called me and said that Rich had cheated death again and was back home. Margaret, who had a large cyst removed from her ovaries, didn't use the pain medication two days after the surgery and recovered much faster than the doctors antici-pated ... all after a friend and I came to the hospital and laid hands on her. All these events make me more confident that I, as a priest, have a unique position in life to help facilitate healing. Maybe it's the power given at ordination, passed down through the centuries. Maybe it is the power of the collar to help people, themselves, believe that God will work miracles in their lives. Maybe it is my belief sys-tem that provides the power. But in any event, I agree with Sarita and Alex, that it is God that is doing the healing. When we align ourselves to this truth, we have salvation of our soul, for we believe that we were created to be whole, healthy, loved and free.

What is your right? You, as a Catholic, as a Christian, as a son or daughter of God, have just as much right to heal and be healed as I do. Yes, because of my position or because of my focus or concentration on this gift, I can facilitate healing maybe at different levels. But you have the power, too. Kathy, a wonderfully loving friend, has empow-ered herself through different techniques and classes to do tremendous healing work, physically, emotionally and Spiritually, on people who have been sent her way. Jacque, because of her willingness to participate in healing on many levels, has now incorporated it with hypnotherapy and Light therapy. This latter technique takes you back to the Light, at which time a full-spectrum lamp is used to ingrain the truths and wisdoms you gathered while being in the Light, back into this present moment. These are "ordinary" people participating in "extraordinary" events. You can heal others with a phone call, a hug, a letter, all coming from sharing unconditional love with the other person. Letting them know that they are worthy to be whole in the sight of all creation. And believe it or not ... no, believe it!, **you** can lay your hands on a person in need of healing and produce a tremendous amount of growth and healing for that per-son. Just for them to know how much you love them by venturing forth to do this, will, at the least, raise their vibration on the Spiritual and emotional levels. Go with God's desires and blessing to use your hands, your heart, to help heal the world. I encourage you also to take a Reiki class. Reiki means Universal Life Force. We would call it God Force, God Love. These classes empower you and initiate you, to a higher level and awareness of hands on healing. There is no religious affiliation connected with these classes. No matter what your name is, or what your position or job in life, Saint Paul tells us in the letter to the Corinthians, "Each one of us does the work the Lord gave us to do: I plant the seed, Apollos watered the plant, but it is God who made the plant grow. There is no difference between the one who plants and the one who waters; God will reward each one according to the work they have done. For we are partners working together for God, and you are God's field." (1 Cor. 3, 5–9) You are a healing partner with God for yourself and for others.

The Body of Christ

Saint Paul also tells us that we are the Body of Christ. When I think of the Holy Communion we receive at Mass, I now think of this Body of Christ in a different way. Knowing that our body is porous and "the space between the atoms," the skin, the people, the planets etc., are all God, then when we hold or take the Eucharist, the Body of Christ, we must mean it when we say "Amen!" Amen, I believe that this body is a part of my body in the same context that you can't separate wine when mixed with water. When you know that you are a part of God now, you **must** heal, you **must** love, you **must** forgive, you **must** set yourself and others free. Once again, Paul says, "You should look on us as Christ's servants who have been put here in charge of God's truth." It is God's truth that you be whole and help others to be whole. You don't need any special tools or techniques like Alex, Jacque, Kathy or myself use. Yes, you can take advantage of those gifts from them to help you along your path. But all you need to be whole is to love others and see that you are worthy of God's love and wholeness for yourself.

Let me tell you a brief story about Phil, about healing by using the tools of laying-on of hands, Eucharist and visualization. Phil is a teacher at the high school. He is about 55 and in the past, he was afflicted with Valley Fever, an illness which sticks with you for many years. He has a deep reverence for the Catholic church and comes to our school-morning Mass which we have every Tuesday and Thursday. One week, after a long bout with the flu and just feeling worn down, he told me he had been to the doctor's and they had found a spot on his lung. They were concerned that it was cancer. He was going to the doctors that morning for further tests. So after communion, I had the other ten people who were present come forth. We placed Phil in the center of our circle and laid our hands on him. I prayed out loud that the Eucharist he had just received would become an acknowledgment of the "holy communion" between him and God. We then asked Jesus, Mary and all his and our guardian angels to be present and heal him so that he could continue serving the Lord in his work at the school. He believed that would help him. I told him I would also have my class pray for him.

When I got to class, I had the kids (seniors) go into a prayerful, meditative state. I had them then visualize a doctor's office as in a white room with an examination table. I told them to see Phil on the table. Next, I had them visualize that the room was beginning to be filled with a bright-white, healing light from God. To see that this light was permeating his lungs. I actually asked the kids to picture that a spot on his lung was dissolving and that new cells were being created. Finally, I had them create a light force around the door. Any doctors or nurses that entered would be effected by this light and would also be instruments of God's healing power.

Well, it so happened that the next day we had an all-school Mass and I hadn't seen Phil yet. After the homily, which happened to be about healing the world through the help of the high school students, I told them that we were praying also for Phil. I told them about the spot on his lung which we were asking God to heal. Phil then stood up and waved to get my attention. He had some good news! The doctors had taken an x-ray and were unable to explain why the spot had disappeared! Miracle? Or do all of you, all of us, simply have the power to connect with God and heal? Both!

On the fourth Sunday of Lent, we read from the Gospel of John about Jesus healing the blind man (Mark 8:22–25). I tell the people after communion that Jesus placed spittle and mud on the blind man's eyes to bring back his sight. I then tell the people, as I tell you, "Think how much more of a healing you are participating in when you receive communion." It is our belief system that we are receiving the Body of Christ. If you know that, then the communion can go straight to your heart, and you can allow yourself to accept its healing power. What a tremendous healing that can accomplish. As we say at the end of Mass, "This Mass is now ended. Go in the peace of Christ to love and serve the Lord, our God." In other words, go in the peace that you have been made whole. You are beautifully whole. Now go and help others be the same. Whether you illicit the powerful tools of a psychic surgeon, visualization, or laying-on of hands, do it for the freedom of your soul. *So be it*!

Chapter Six

The Gathering of the Four Races

"The Return of the Rainbow"

J acque and Sacred Life Association once again became another bridge leading from old territory to new. Jacque attended the World Spiritual Leaders Summit Conference in Rio de Janerio in 1991. At this summit, she met many Spiritual masters, among them, David Crouchain, the leader of the Ojibway Indian tribe in Manitoba, Canada. Both David and Jacque shared their dreams and visions with the people at the conference. They came to find out that they had a common vision: The Gathering of the Four Races. The long awaited communion of the white, black, red and yellow people coming together as one circle. So David and Jacque began to implement this dream by creating their own gathering, their own conference of the Four Races. This gathering would take place on the land of the Ojibway people in a cold, desolate lodge in faraway Manitoba, Canada.

The call came through the church rectory, and I heard an excited Jacque on the other end of the line. She breathlessly told me about her Spiritual experiences in Rio and how she

had met a "holy man." Not only was she attracted to him
on a personal level, but she saw him as one who stood as
a great warrior and visionary for his people. As if she had
just found a long-lost friend, Jacque shared with me how his
vision had paralleled her own vision. A vision of our future
world soon-to-be reunited. "You have to come with our
group to share in this message and find out how it fits into
your own ministry," she pleaded. I quickly said yes, knowing that God is always finding us new adventures and new
horizons to encounter Beauty. I checked out the upcoming
church events and "just my luck!" it turned out that nothing of major importance was happening that would keep me
tied to the parish. So off I went again on another foreign
adventure to a remote, new horizon. What barriers would
I break through this time? What Beauty would I discover?

It was the winter of 1993 and in Canada, winter is really
winter for this California boy. The temperature was way
below zero and the wind was biting this pioneer's face
harshly when we stepped out of the airport. We attempted
to maneuver the roads out to a distant lodge where the
gathering was to be held. When we got closer to the loca-
tion, the snow and wind stopped and we could see a very
flat countryside with stubbles of corn or wheat shafts speck-
ling the fields. I heard that some members of Sacred Life
Association were going to donate some buffalo to these
people. Could any buffalo survive out here? How could
people survive in this cold? As we approached the lodge, I
saw a tall teepee with black smoke coming out of its top.
"Well, at least there is fire to keep warm," I said, as the car
engine died in the cold.

No one was outside to greet us except a young boy with
a huge smile, dressed in a large, warm parka. He gave
Jacque a big bear hug. It turned out that this young boy was
the son of the leader of the conference and had met Jacque
at some of the planning meetings. The rest of us followed
the leader, hoping for the best in guessing about the inte-
rior of the lodge. Much to our relief, a blast of warm air hit

us as we entered the front door. There was light, voices and laughter. The hall still had some Christmas decorations up, mainly for the benefit of the young children, as these indigenous people didn't celebrate a traditional Christmas. But these familiar trimmings took some of the nervous edge out of the air. I was nervous about how these indigenous people would greet this "white man." Much to our delight, a married couple, Dwanne and Shirley, greeted us, dressed in their full Native American attire. Seeing these two people stand so tall and proud (despite the fact that Shirley is in a wheelchair!), spoke to me, as though in picture form, of their history and lore. I knew I was going to be in for an adventure and an expansion of my mind. (Dwanne and Shirley are pictured in their costumes on page 152.)

In sharing a meal with our hosts, I discovered that they were as nervous as I was. Who were we? Where were we from? What race? They were extremely open and friendly. All looked forward to the exchange of ideas and beliefs. Most of the younger kids, early teens and younger, had discovered that I was a Catholic priest. A barrage of questions came flying at me. "Where's your priest outfit?" "How can you be here at this gathering?" "Isn't it against the church to be here at this type of gathering?" "What will your people say?" And of course, "Why can't you get married?" and "What's it like hearing confessions?" I just smiled and tried to tell them about "my culture," the church, in the best terms that I could. I asked a lot of questions myself. "What are all those animals, stuffed or pictured, around the walls?"

"They are sacred animals, representing sacred truths," they responded.

"What are all the colored strips of cloth tied to the tree set up in the middle of the room?"

They looked at me as though I was so ignorant! They laughed and grinned broadly. "They represent the colors of the four races: black, yellow, white and red," they answered with delight, becoming the new teachers to a Catholic priest. I chuckled inside, thinking how the tables had turned!

Dwanne
&
Shirley

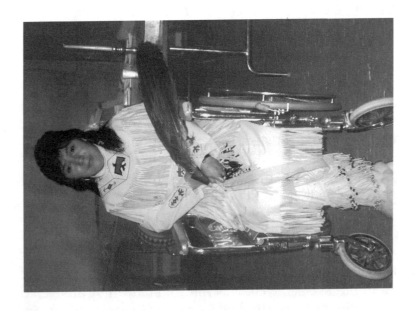

After dinner the opening talks were to begin. However, I noticed that everyone was setting up for a pipe ceremony. I was familiar with pipe ceremonies as Jacque and many other of the Sacred Life members had been gifted a pipe and had done ceremonies in San Diego. Earlier, I had read an excellent book called *The Breath of the Invisible*, by John Redtail Freesoul. This book carefully and clearly spells out the parts, purpose and traditions of the pipe and ceremony. Tradition says that the Native American people were gifted the pipe by a Spirit Woman, White Buffalo Calf Woman, and told that the smoke symbolized their connection (their prayer, if you will) with the Spirit world. (Many have said this Spirit Woman's presentation of the pipe is similar to Moses bringing the Ten Commandments.) The Spirit world was represented by the Grandfathers and Grandmothers. During the ceremony, they honor all the earth by smoking to the four directions. Each direction is also portrayed by a sacred animal, the eagle, hawk, bear and buffalo. Each direction represents something very important in our Spiritual journey. East is where the sun rises, where we receive enlightenment. This is the place of new beginnings, springtime, the infant stage of our life, where we are open to growth. The golden eagle is its spiritual animal. The eagle flies high and is the messenger of dreams and visions. South continues the spiritual journey of the youth. As in the summertime, there is rapid growth associated with this direction. The redtail hawk is the animal of the South. It is a fearless hunter and swift flyer in the winds of life, never to be harmed as it is balanced and in harmony. The rose, the plant of this direction, is a reflection of the redtail hawk. It is protected from harm by its thorns, while still budding forth its beauty. West is the new horizon and always beckons us, as pioneers, to broaden our horizons. It also carries with it the symbol of the sunset. Here, one is called, like an adult in midlife, to introspection for maturing purposes. It is a time to prepare for the new horizon of elderhood. The bear is associated with this direction and symbolizes not only gentleness in its natural environments, but also strength and courage to stand tall and forthright on a new path or when confronted with danger. Finally, North is the medicine of relaxation into "old age" along with a heightened awareness of new, renewed adventures into the spirit realm. This is a time for objectivity, where you are able to see the "forest for the trees" and *vice versa*. The White Buffalo is the proud animal of this direction. This sacred buffalo is there to nourish all people, spiritually, physically, and emotionally. I encourage you to read more about this subject. It is fascinating and can teach you many new ways to deepen your relationship with God and heighten your awareness of God's presence through so many directions beyond that which we have been told.

Included in this ceremony are prayers to our Spirit guides, equivalent to saints and angels for Catholics and other Christians. And prayers to loved ones who have passed on, as well as a time to pray for those who are ill and in need of God and Spirit to help them. All this is very similar to our traditional prayers. We pray and dialog with our loved ones who have died and transformed into Spirit. We have been taught to pray for those who are in need of God's healing. AND, any Catholic can tell you about the use of smoke, that is, incense, during our liturgies. Incense is very biblical. The 30th chapter of the book of Exodus, verses one through ten, speaks specifically about how to set up an altar of incense. In the New Testament, at the time when Zechariah (father of John the Baptist) was offering incense in the Temple, the angel Gabriel appeared to him. Since biblical times and the fading of paganism, incense has been used by the church as a mark of respect and blessing for gifts brought up during Mass, the ministers, altars and the faithful. It is also incorporated at the end of a funeral service as a sign of our prayers rising upward to heaven to ask the assistance of God and angels to help in this time of need. This assistance is not only for us "left behind," but also for those who are on the new journey in Spirit. So, in conjunction with my familiarity with this use of smoke/incense from our tradition, as well as from my own personal experiences with the pipe, I was ready to sit right down and participate in this blessing of the opening of the Gathering of the Four Races.

David Crouchain, leader of this particular Ojibway tribe, stood proudly before the gathering of people. He welcomed all representative peoples of the four races. On one side of him sat Jacque, adorned with traditional Native American jewelry (her mother's side of the family is Cherokee), and on the other, the Ojibway's Elder and Medicine Man, Albert Land. (On Page 156 is a picture of David Crouchain, the author, Albert Land and Jacque Snyder.) I had seen a picture of David on the wall, along with his father and his grandfather. Each was wearing a ceremonial buffalo head with horns. I knew David carried within him great wisdom about our earth, our world, its people and where we were headed. He said, "Boozhoo" ... Welcome! "I am Red Thunder Bear-Who-Walks; I am Blue Kind-Hearted Man; I am White Eagle Man; I am Person with an Elder Spirit. I am of Bear Clan; Eagle is my Spirit; I am Horse Warrior." As he spoke each one of these names, I could see around him and above him a visual of what each one represented. First he told us of the anger his people had towards the white people for trampling their traditions, people, land, and animals. But that is now gone, he said. Now was a time to look forward and to let go of the past. He pledged for himself and for his people to focus on his visions and the visions of the elders which spoke of the four races coming together in peace. From that point on, his talk was all positive. This put a lot of us at ease, for there had been some fear that all we would hear was "white man bashing." God is good! David then went on to quote a famed and well known leader of Indian people named Crazy Horse, who well over a hundred years ago talked of a gathering.

David Crouchain, "myself," Albert Land and
Jacque Snyder

The great Spirit would make the whole earth one circle, and men of honor would take the place of dishonor. It was to be a time when the earth would be made beautiful again, and the two-leggeds, the four-leggeds, the winged, and all living things would find new life in Beauty.

Red Thunder Bear Who Walks (David) spoke with pride, knowing he was sharing with us, his and our responsibility to bring this dream alive. He said that Crazy Horse foresaw this gathering of the white race, the black race, the red race and the yellow race as he quoted,

> I see a time, after the sky has grown dark and ugly and the waters bad-smelling, when the young white ones will come to those of our people who still carry the spark of knowledge of unity with all that lives and ask for freedom. In that day, there will be some who carry the light and who will give it to them.

My purpose in sharing this chapter with you about the Gathering is twofold. First of all, we need to acknowledge that the indigenous people, the *Native*, original people of this land, long before we came to Christianize them, drive them from their land and take away their buffalo, had answers that would one day help us all get back to a way of life and belief system of who we are. We would once again show respect to the earth, God and one another. So we need to learn from these people. We need to see the Beauty in their heritage and teachings. Yes, they have made mistakes along the way ... so have we, so has the church. But they hold valuable information about our future and how we can live to get there. Take time to learn about these ways. Take up some of the practices you read about in this chapter. Integrate them into your lives so as to enhance your Beauty, the God within you. Keep an open mind as you read on and learn how God works through many marvelous and mysterious ways.

The second purpose for including this chapter, as with all the chapters in this book, is to empower you. Whatever race you are a part of, know the powerful influence you can have in assuming your God-given role in the stewardship of this planet. As this world cleans up and becomes the paradise that I believe it will become, it needs you to listen, learn and implement the wisdoms that have been afforded you. YOU are important. David summarized his powerful talk to us (and to YOU!) by quoting Fools Crow, a holy man and ceremonial chief of the Teton Sioux.

> Whenever it is possible, when I am doing my ceremonies, I put my black flag here (West) ... red flag here (North) ... yellow flag over here (East) ... white flag over here (South). These are the Spiritual representatives of all races, and they remind me that Grandfather Spirits serve others as well as the Indian. We are the keepers of certain areas of knowledge, which we are to share for the good of mankind. And the blacks and the Orientals and whites are each keepers of knowledge that can and should be used to benefit us.

If all that wasn't enough to make us get up and go out into the world and work overtime or double time in helping create heaven on earth, David told a magnificent story about an encounter he had with Jesus in a dream. He realized the man in his dream was a messenger with a powerful message. David saw him wearing a robe tied at his waist and his hair was shoulder length. He began to cry in astonishment, realizing it was Jesus who was appearing before him. The message, he said, was long and detailed, but the one thing he remembered most was that Jesus said, "Go and find my people." He took this to mean to gather the people together from all the races and gather all their wisdom, their teachings of old and new, and bring together the common messages to show people how they can change the world. This was a very powerful message with which to end the night. He encouraged us to slumber well and to travel afar in our dreams, and come back knowing that we are the people whom this vision spoke of.

The next morning, we all returned to the lodge refreshed and renewed. It was now our time to stand up and share, as people from all the different races, our stories and visions. I was honored to come before these people and tell them I was a Catholic priest who worked hard to hold the vision of God's covenant with his people. I told how Christian people need to be seen as people who are also on the journey. "My people" are a people who deeply desire peace and harmony between all people. In my ministry with the people of my parish, I have learned how deeply they desire to learn more about God and the dream God had for us. We share in the Sacrament of Reconciliation, a visible sign of God, as the Indians see smoke being such in their pipe ceremony. This Sacrament of Reconciliation helps those who missed the mark and needed to re-center themselves. We have the Sacrament of Confirmation for the youth moving into adulthood, to re-affirm their important role in the church. Our Eucharist of bread and wine is for those desiring to be nourished in greater ways by God. Prayer and retreats for those on the journey provide private time and solitude to find more of themselves in relationship with God. All the pain and terror the churches imposed on native people years ago must be healed by understanding and accepting the fact that there are many good, searching, compassionate people in our churches today. Most of all, I told those present how I would take back the messages from this Gathering and talk about the importance of "this Gathering" with my people during Mass, at school, at Youth Group, at Senior Citizen gatherings and amongst my brother priests. I asked that they also include the people of the church in their circle of life, in their prayers and in their hope. I remembered the quote from Catholic theologian, Pierre Teilhard de Chardin who said,

We have just entered upon the greatest period of change the world has ever known. We have reached a crossroads in human evolution where the only road which leads forward is toward a common passion. In spite of all the apparent improbabilities, a fresh kind of life is starting.

The words "common passion" rang in my ears and heart. I asked those gathered to open themselves up to new understandings of all people, just as I ask our people at church to understand the way of the indigenous people. Yes, common passion is important, but it is even more important to shift our focus to the reality that we are a common family. "Amen," I told them. "Amen ... we must believe."

New Lessons

David stood up and spoke before the group once again. He wished to tell us about the Seven Sacred Teachings of his people. These were handed down by the grandfathers to keep the people close to God through the earth and all its creations. The seven teachings are respect, love, courage, honesty, wisdom, humility and truth. The teachings were told through, and connected with, animals. I already mentioned that animals were important in the pipe ceremonies. Now we will see how they use them to teach their sacred wisdoms. As you read each one of these, attempt to feel which teaching pulls on your heart strings. Is this the lesson you are working on most in life? Or is this the one you have managed to integrate into your life the best? The one you relate to most may also be your warrior clan or Spirit clan animal. More on that fascinating subject later!

The first teaching David told us about was **Respect**. Respect is seen as Grandfather Buffalo. The buffalo was very much respected by his people because the buffalo gave his whole being, every part of it, for his people to live. The buffalo's meat and flesh were used for food. The hide was made into warm clothing. By this sacrifice, he became sacred. Much like Jesus, the buffalo teaches to give of yourself and never to expect anything in return. Your reward shall not only be great in heaven but also on earth.

The teaching of **Love** is associated with the Grandfather Eagle. Flying the highest in the skies, the eagle is the one closest to the Creator. He is the most sacred bird of the native people. In his flight, he carries our prayers to the Creator. It is because of his love that he becomes a messenger for his people. Many times, you can become like the eagle and pray for those in need. In your prayers for yourself or others, observe the eagle, the dove or the Holy Spirit with wings, take your prayers to the highest heights of the Divine.

Grandfather Bear carries the teaching of **Courage**. Unlike common misconceptions of bears being fierce and destructive, for the native people, bear is brother to the people. Grandfather Bear exhibits no fear and only strength. The bear gives of himself by fasting through the winter for his people. The bear gives us dreams and visions for purpose in our lives. The bear is the caretaker and protector of Mother Earth. Imagine what courage you would find in standing up for the truth if you pictured yourself with a bear skin around you? Could you fathom anyone not being just a little bit more willing to listen to your message? Know that God's Spirit of courage, whatever form it takes, is always with you.

Honesty is a teaching that carries with it an interesting animal. This animal is called Sabe (saw-bay). We know it as Bigfoot. This big animal is very revered by the native people and carries with him great medicine. He appears to them in both physical and Spiritual form ... and please do believe this, they are being completely honest! The more honesty within, the bigger your Spirit is. Honesty is always telling the truth, never fabricating a nontruth, a lie. Jesus, bigger than life, said firmly, "State the truth and the truth shall set you free."

Have any of these touched your heart yet? Try this one. Here's one we all could emulate. This teaching of **Wisdom** is carried by the beaver. The beaver shows his wisdom by wisely using his gifts given to him by God, the Creator. In life, if the beaver didn't use his gifts, he would die. But the beaver, like all of us need to do, brings lifeless areas to life when he uses his gifts and talents. He shows wisdom also by picking areas that will require the use of his gifts. So often, we spin our wheels trying to "grow" where there is no chance of growth. Trying to help people who just don't want help! Working in jobs that are not using our gifts and talents. With faith in God, you can use your wisdoms where and with whom you are needed and grow and prosper in the process.

Humility is brought to us by the wolf. When a wolf hunts, it is not primarily for himself. He hunts to feed the young ones first, the older, then the sick. He thinks of himself last. In a wolf pack, the wolf has only one leader and the wolf humbles himself to follow the leader of his pack. Our Master Jesus said, "If you want to be first, you must serve others." Are you humble enough to stop thinking of yourself for just one minute? Service of others is the ultimate Spiritual gift you can attain.

Finally we have the teaching of **Truth**. Turtle, the one who has been there since time began, carries the original instructions of life given by God. Learn from the turtle and go within yourself to find the truth. It will be the greatest journey you have ever taken.

I would like to suggest that you buy *The Medicine Cards* by James Sams and David Carson. These are wonderful cards and excellent lessons which can help you open a new window to see God and God's truths in our lives. I have used these on retreats with seniors in high school and they loved this new learning device. It was amazing to see how many picked just the right animal. On the back of the card, I had printed the explanation of the lesson and much to their surprise, it was just the confirmation they needed to hear. The understanding of these beautiful creations of God can greatly improve your relationship with God and empower you on your own Spiritual journey. You can use these in your daily meditations or whenever one of these animals crosses your path, so to speak.

One night a friend and I were standing outside on a balcony gazing at all the marvelous stars in the sky. Behind us we heard the hooting of an owl. After standing quietly and enjoying the owl's soothing music, the owl flew away. We hurried back into the house to look up its meaning in the Medicine Card book. Owl was reminding us both in our own personal journeys and work environments to use our powers, to be silent observers of things going on around us, as though using the owl's night vision. Its medicine emphasized that we should pay close attention to our messages in the night in forms of dreams or meditations. We needed to know again that by using this insight, no one can deceive us about what they are doing.

Another day, I was outside and a hawk flew right by me. The book told me this animal's medicine came by to remind me to be observant of life all around. Life is magical, hawk says. This magic can overcome any stressful or difficult situations. Get a higher perspective on life! Boy did *I* ever need that message at that particular time in life. I had become too bogged down with some of the dramas in my life and was also going through some very complicated transitions with the church and my assignments. Thank you God for all your wonderful messengers in life.

Healing Ceremonies, Medicine, Names and Clans

As the sun set over the frozen tundra and hearty dinner conversations came to an end, a circle of chairs was set up in the middle of the lodge. Albert, the Medicine Man, stood to address the gatherers. He spoke of a vision Spirit had given him. It was a vision for the world. One day, Spirit told him, he and three other people would take a journey into the woods and deep forests. There Spirit would direct them as to which plants, herbs and roots to pick. From this collection would come all the healing medicines for every illness in the world. A miracle from God. "But," he lamented, "the time had not yet come for this journey. Therefore, we must rely on our traditional healing circles with grandfather and grandmother Spirits to help us."

So he asked all those in need of healing to sit in this circle of chairs and pray to be healed. Many of the Indian men, as well as some women, came and stood behind these people. They carried with them rattles and feathers, and soon began to shake the rattle over and around the person in need. The feathers were used to dust off negativity. As though silently directed by Spirit, they all ended at the same time. The next group in need of healing, either emotionally, psychically or mentally, came forth. Jacque had been one of those doing the healing and she signaled me to come stand behind a man to work on healing him. I was handed a rattle and feather. I have to admit, I was a little nervous. I wondered what a Native American would think about a Catholic priest participating in his healing. But I only received unconditional acceptance from him. When the healing time began, I prayed just as I would when I traditionally laid my hands on someone who would call me to do so as a priest. I was in a bit of a quandary as what to do with the rattle and feather. So I asked God to use my hands to heal as Jesus did. After shaking the rattle around this man and using the feather as though dusting off negativity, I laid my hands on his shoulders and continued to pray for a healing. He told me afterward that my hands were very hot and he felt as though "something" lifted off him during the whole process. "I feel very much better, thank you!" Hmm, imagine that! A Catholic priest in a Native American lodge praying to Spirit for a healing. I just heard a voice within me say, "With God, nothing is impossible." Maybe I did have a special place among these people. Maybe Native Spirituality was to have meaning in my life.

David then came out of the darkness and explained about Indian names and Spirit and Warrior clans. They believe that each person also has an Indian name, given to them by Spirit. This sounded like the old Catholic practice of a child choosing a saint's name before being baptized. David has many names but the first name he was given was Red Thunder Bear Who Walks. These represent something special to each person. Each person also has a Warrior and a Spiritual clan associated with him which could help him or her to more deeply understand their relationship with God in life. The seven Sacred Animals mentioned in the seven Sacred Teachings are usually the ones named in the clan names. However, your Indian name can come from an animal different than the seven Sacred Animals. Let me use myself as an example. A tall young man named Wayne stood behind me in prayer to have a name delivered through him. (Sounds like channeling or speaking in tongues to me!) I had learned earlier that Wayne was a Spiritual young man who had chosen to follow the traditional ways of his people despite many obstacles which he had to overcome. He took up his position as a warrior and a great healer. He had been in several sun dances. At these, he had been "pierced." He dragged the buffalo skulls pierced to his back in several ceremonies. I could feel his Spiritual presence behind me reaching far beyond his physical dimensions.

After a long prayerful silence, Wayne stepped back and smiled. He said that I was all wolf clan. I was Timber Wolf Warrior Clan: "Mian Okichita." I was Wolf Spirit Clan: "Maigun Doodame." My Indian name was "Pimashet Wapshki Mistettim:" Flying White Horse Man. "Flying White Horse Man," I thought. "Flying White Horse! Holy Mackerel!" I had a flashback to a time when I was on an inner shamanic journey a few years earlier. I was attempting to discover my power animals. In the shamanic world of inner journeying, these animals are ones who help you journey and learn more about yourself and God. It came to me that my power animal was a two-headed flying white horse. Whenever I went on one of those journeys, I would call my animal. I would grab onto its mane and fly to wherever I needed to go, to learn. Now to have this confirmation and be called Flying White Horse Man. God is alive! Spirit will do anything to make us see that God is presence in all ways, all races, all people, all things.

When I went back to my room that night, I took some time to meditate on my wolf clan. Wolf came to me and said that it was to teach me more about myself. "Be like the wolf clan to which you belong. Wolves are leaders, as you are. Wolves never look back. Bay to the moon ... Cry to the light in all things ... See the light reflected in everyone, as the moon reflects the light of the sun. Use your eyes keenly. Watch out for traps set to capture you. Outsmart the hunter. Search for new horizons. Take care of others in your pack." Each time I closed my eyes, I saw, and still do see in ceremonies, the wolf smiling before me, snuggling up to me.

For a few moments, things went blank and black for me during my meditation. I was still soaking up the goodness of my wolf friends. Then, out of nowhere, with my eyes still closed, I saw before me a beautiful Indian chief on a white horse. He was dressed in white buckskin, with a full headdress of feathers flowing down his shoulders over the side of the horse nearly touching the ground. He had a long staff in his hand with white feathers flowing from it. I was in awe of this beautiful man. I felt as though he was standing right before me. Then he simply and plainly said, "Now is the time to come out of the wilderness." He turned and disappeared into the dark. I was flabbergasted, blown away. I have rarely had a vision as clear as this one. It held the clarity of my vision of Jesus and Mary in Mexico as described in the chapter about the pyramids. Although I "knew" what he was saying, it was as though I was trying to fool myself as I fell into slumber, thinking, "What did he mean, 'Now is the time to come out of the wilderness?'"

I couldn't wait to find David or Wayne and ask them if they knew who this warrior was. Neither could be found during breakfast and the butterflies inside me increased with anticipation. Eventually, they both walked through the door with Jacque and I rushed up to ask them. Jacque smiled as I described the scenario. She knew who he was for she had seen him before in one of her meditations. David looked at me in surprise. "Why that's Onyate, an ancient Spiritual warrior. He doesn't 'show up' too often so you had better pay attention to what he has to say!"

Now I knew exactly what Onyate was trying to say to me. No more pussyfooting around. No more fear. No more hesitation. Come out from the shadows and speak the truth of God. Stand in the light and proclaim equality for all peoples without prejudice of race, color, gender, sexual preference, political affiliation or whatever.

Truth comes from the Native Americans, from Catholics, from Hindus, from the rain forests of the Amazons. Truth is in all people's hearts. As for me personally, I was being called to be a beacon of God's light and love to people in the church who were willing and open to break out of outdated beliefs. I was challenged to speak from my heart, as Jesus always spoke from his sacred heart, and tell people to lift their chins and look straight ahead into the eyes of another human being and know they are seeing the eyes of God. I echo Onyate's words to others to come out of their own self-imposed wilderness, however that was created. To join a people of many colors, many backgrounds, many traditions, in proclaiming that this earth is alive and we must treat it and each other with dignity.

Our bible has a wonderful story to remind us of this message that we are to be in the sunlight and no longer live in fear-filled wildernesses, storms or isolation. It comes from Genesis 9:9–13. These are the words God spoke to Noah:

> God said, "See, I am now establishing my covenant with you and your descendants after you and with every living creature that is with you. I will establish my covenant with you, that never again shall all bodily creatures be destroyed by the waters of a flood; there shall not be another flood to devastate the earth ... This is the sign that I am giving for all ages to come, of the covenant between me and you and every living creature with you:

I set my rainbow in the clouds
to serve as a sign of the covenant
between me and the earth.

We are a Rainbow People. We are here to live life as the true heirs of the kingdom of God on Earth. It is vital to know that it has been the Native American people who kept many of the messages of truth alive through their traditional beliefs. Let us not be blind to these ways. Open your hearts and minds and eyes to learn more about these ways. **Pay heed to this story** ...

A small boy, walking down the street one bright summer day, spotted a copper penny glistening at his feet. He picked it up and clutched it protectively. He felt a glow of pride and excitement. It was his, and it cost him nothing! From that day on, wherever he went, he walked with his head down, eyes surveying the ground for more treasures. During his lifetime, he found 302 pennies, 24 nickels, 41 dimes, 8 quarters, 3 half dollars, and one worn out paper dollar—a total of $12.82. The money had cost him nothing -- except that he missed the breathless Beauty of 35,127 sunsets, the colorful splendor of 327 rainbows, the brilliance of hundreds of maples nipped by the autumn frost, babies growing, white clouds floating across the crystal sky, birds flying, animals running, sun shining and the countless smiles of passing people.

My friends, it's time to wake up and look up and *Come out of the wilderness* and be the people, the new race of Love, that we are all called to be.

Sunday Sermons

This sermon/homily was given in Advent, the time before Christmas. I place this after the chapter on "The Gathering of the Four Races" which draws on oneness, peace and harmony. As you will see, I sing a song near the end of this homily. I sang sometimes during my homilies for two reasons: (1) I like to do the outrageous, the unexpected, that which will make the people perk up and listen; (2) I believe that a vibration comes with singing, which (combined with my love for the people) touches the heart area (chakra) and facilitates the potential to open and awaken their divinity.

The scientist tells us that there are as many as 100,000 planets out there where life could have developed and probably has. The chances are better than not that there are other civilizations out there ... perhaps more rational or intelligent than we are. Now ... why haven't they contacted us? Well, there are several potential answers or possibilities. The first one is obvious: **The distance is too great.** The nearest star to our sun is twenty-two million light years away. The second theory is that **the life that exists in these unknown islands of space might still be in a primitive state.** Something like our own Ice Age or those times when we lived in caves. The third reason is that **our neighboring civilizations are now extinct**. They have gone through some kind of life cycle: birth, growth and death. They have lived for many ages of what we call time, but they are no more. Now, the fourth theory as to why other races, other civilizations in space, do not make contact with us is a chilling one. That reason being **because they don't want to come into contact with us!** They prefer to stay at a distance ... quarantined, so to speak. They have seen us and they recoil at what they see. They see violence and our capacity to destroy one another. They see us invent an airplane which can conquer distances, and they see us use it to drop bombs and kill millions. They see too much prejudice and disunity. They don't see enough peace on earth and love which fills our hearts. And perhaps seeing all this, they want no part of us.

These are very sobering thoughts which I'm sure we don't want to live with. But how can we believe we will change? Is there any sign that we can live in hope and peace?

"Ask for a sign from the Lord," said the prophet.
"And this is the sign he will give you:
The virgin shall be with child and bear a son
and he will be called Emmanuel."

There was a conversation once between a Jew and a Christian. The Jewish person speaks first: "Unlike you, I still wait for a messiah. But with the world so evil, I don't understand why he has not come." And the Christian answers: "Unlike you, I believe that the Messiah has come, but I don't understand why, then, the world continues to be so evil!"

I seemed to be obsessed with the thinking this Christmas season that we must not only celebrate his birth, but also his truth and life. Peace on earth isn't just for December 25th, but also for always. To get across that point, I would like to share with you a story. A true story of another Christmas long ago, more than 100 years ago, back in 1870 in the midst of the Franco-Prussian war ... one of the many wars between France and Germany. It was Christmas Eve and the war was being fought on the outskirts of Paris. It was cold that night and the men involved in that terrible battle were thinking of their loved ones they'd left at home. All about them were the sounds of the battle, of the cannons, of men dying. Then all of a sudden, a young French soldier climbed out of the trenches and stood there ... an open target on the battlefield. He began to sing this old French carol: (*I then sang the following.*)

O, Holy night, the stars are brightly shining,
it is the night of our dear Savior's birth.
Long lay the world in sin and error pining
'til he appeared and soul felt its worth.
A thrill of hope, the weary world rejoices,
for yonder breaks a new and glorious morn'.
Fall on your knees, O hear the angels' voices,
O night divine, O night when Christ was born,
O night divine, O night when Christ was born.

(*Dramatic pause.*) And a silence settled on the battlefield as soldiers from both sides listened. Then when the French soldier finished singing, a German soldier climbed out of his trench and answered that French carol with a German Christmas song. And again, there was peace and silence on the battlefield as the soldiers reflected on the message of peace which Christmas meant.
Eventually, and unfortunately, the battle would

begin again and more men would die that night. But for a few moments, the Spirit of peace on earth and good will to all silenced the guns, the cannons, the hatred ... such was the power of Christmas.

Wouldn't it be great if we could have peace every day in our lives instead of on just Christmas Eve or Christmas day? Wouldn't it be great if that spaceship could come down from the sky and see no hatred or bitterness or war on this earth. It can happen if we start every day to live the truth of Jesus Christ ... yes, the answer is still Christ, but the Christ within us. That is the meaning of his title, the special name we hear today: "Emmanuel ... God with us." So let's start Christmas early this season and let's make it last all year long by having peace on earth and good will toward all people. *Amen.*

Chapter Seven
Back on
"The Path"
"Living the Beauty"

*"On that same day, two of them were going to a village
named Emmaus, about seven miles from Jerusalem,
and they were talking to each other
about all the things that had happened.
As they talked and discussed, Jesus himself drew near
and walked along with them; they saw him,
but somehow did not recognize him."*
Luke 24:13-16 **The Road to Emmaus**

All right, you have traveled to five different horizons! I am sure some of your beliefs may have been stretched beyond what you thought they could. But you made it. You have seen that, "Yes, God does speak to me ... God does channel information to me that is very helpful in my life." If you really take a look at your Spiritual life, you may find that you have been an open channel of God all along. Now you are seeing that exercised through another window. You also were exposed to a radical form of healing. Psychic surgery did not blow you out of the water, but put you back in touch with the reality that we all can create healing in our lives or others' lives in some way or another. Learning that one man, Alex Orbito, can actually enter another's body with the prayerful use of his God-guided hands does something to you on a spiritual level. God does heal in very mysterious ways. So can you! Seeing was believing for me. Reincarnation may have been the hardest horizon for many of you to cross over and survey. But allowing the mind another area to play within brings about greater understanding to long-term patterns that have plagued us with no foreseeable solutions. Just fantasizing about how all these patterns got started in past lives will bring about some healing and growth in your life. Your world is a far greater, larger world because of your courage. Expanding your world to adventure with me on my journeys to the pyramids at Teo was a way that you could be a part of the party being lead by Miguel. It was very similar, I am sure, to walking with Jesus in his time as he pointed out new perspectives, new ways of life. Hopefully these encounters and horizons have spurred you on to discuss with others, as the Gospel of Luke says, "All the things that had happened." It is a natural desire of God to have things discussed about God when you are on your Sacred Pathway.

The four chapters about channeling, reincarnation, Teotihuacan and psychic surgery are reminders to you that you are on a common path: you are a Spiritual being on a human pathway. That pathway must become Sacred because of who you are. You are a channel of God! You are the earthen vessels. You are here this lifetime to get it right, to accept your divinity and not get caught up in all this world's illusions. You have the keys of understanding a healthier, happier, holier way.

We turn back to the prophecies of old that tell us "the circle shall be closed." The four races, all the races, shall come together and work for one people, one truth and one way, the way of love. With this perspective, you can be like the disciples on the road to Emmaus. You can know that the Christ and your Christedness are bringing it all together.

And Jesus explained to them what was said about him in all the Scriptures, beginning with the books of Moses and the writings of the prophets.

... So he went in to stay with them. He sat at table with them, took the bread, and said the blessing, then he broke the bread and gave it to them. Their eyes were opened and they recognized him; but he disappeared from their sight. They said to each other, "Wasn't it like a fire burning in us when he talked to us on the road and explained the Scriptures to us?"

They got up at once and went back to Jerusalem, where they found the eleven disciples gathered together with the others ... The two then explained to them what had happened on the road, and how they had recognized the Lord when he broke the bread. (Luke 24.17–35)

Look back on your path and see how God has been interwoven in YOUR life all along. See how God and the Spirit of God within YOU have taken seriously the responsibility of making this earth a kingdom as it should be, as it is in what we call heaven. Just by the fact that you have read this book you are participating in that building of the kingdom. There are no boundaries to or in this kingdom. There is room enough for everyone. And the kingdom is supposed to grow and grow and grow, for that is what God does. Many of the books at this present time are stating that we are at a very critical period in our planet's evolution. Because of the state this world is in and because there are so many people who are ready to take a leap in life, the prophecies and predictions about an imminent change in this world appear very true. All the more reason for you to realize that you are called to a path of light and love, a pathway far greater expanded upon than you have ever travelled before. Participate in this Beauty. The seriousness of this task is commanding you to get back on the path and honor it and all you have learned along the way. Do not fear that the demand is too great. Consider it an honor. Consider it a joy. Consider it a "Love Task" you chose to accomplish with God long ago. The path is yours!

Chapter Eight
The Age of the Innocent
"The Omega and the Alpha: the End and the Beginning"

he innocent. The one who dreams and always hopes dreams can come true. The one who is the first to jump with glee at the sight of an evening star, a white horse, a four-leaf clover. The innocent is the one who believes that the Kingdom of God can be a reality in the here and now. There are a lot of us innocents out there. It's a blessing and a curse.

The blessing. It's the side of us that sees the good in everything, as Jesus saw the good in Mary Magdelene. *The curse.* Some people call us Pollyanna, or someone who sees through rose-colored glasses. Either way, the innocent is a child at heart. I was one of those people. I believe I still am.

My exploration through new doors and onto new horizons into the New Age areas played a major role in my life, in the priesthood and my transition. The encounters with Sarita, Elisabeth Kübler-Ross, Adele Tinning and many other people as time unfolded kept me balanced. These new adventures strengthened my foundational belief in a God who loved us, period, without any rules and regulations, except the rule of love. I would try to integrate these new concepts into my teachings with the people at the parish or whenever giving a retreat. However, I couldn't come right out and say, "Well, I was channeling Joshua the other day." Or "I saw this great healing take place as I saw Alex put his hand into someone's stomach!" It would have been difficult to say in the confessional, "Maybe this is due to a past-life connection!"

I remember talking with Dolores Cannon one time about her books. She wrote about a woman who had a past-life as an Essene teacher to Jesus." She asked me if I used any of this material in my work in the church and how. I said, "Yes, I do ... and I do it very carefully!" I wanted to stand up in the pulpit and say, "Hey, I know this woman who has a client who taught Jesus almost 2000 years ago and learned such and such." But I couldn't. I did think about what it would be like to hear this conversation and sometimes I would write my homilies in such a dialog fashion. As you can tell from all the information presented in the past chapters, there was so much to share. Yet I felt like an attorney, slapped with a gag order. "Don't even think about entering that area or talking about that!" So like a clever attorney, I had to find other ways to get my point across.

With all these broader New Age understandings of God lurking in my mind, I continued to find new ways of expressing God. I created innovative ways to bring the grace of God to the people. I climbed up a ladder one Sunday and read from Shel Silverstein's, *The Giving Tree*, a story about God's unconditional, ever-giving love for us all. I used the ladder *motive* in another parish, leaning it up against the statue of the Blessed Mother Mary. I pulled a letter out from behind the statue (which I had placed there earlier) and "pretended" it was a loving note from her son, Jesus, which he had written just before his crucifixion ordeal. It told her/us not to worry because only love, forgiveness and understanding counted. I used fog at one reconciliation service to show them how they needed to come "out of the fog," into the light, forget their sins and accept God's love. I sang songs from my favorite musical shows, *The Phantom of the Opera, Cats, Les Miserables* and others, to touch the people in other vibrational ways. Often times, I had people close their eyes and we would do a short meditation, either talking with God, Jesus, Mary or a guardian angel. And I wanted them to know that they had the power to heal, too. After communion, I would have them close their eyes again and send this divine presence within them out to others in need.

I could see that many people were touched or moved by these different ways to deliver the powerful message of God's love. Sometimes I would see people with tears in their eyes. Often times I saw smiles and heard laughter, something not accepted in the old traditional ways. I felt joy in the tones of the people's conversations after Mass. Yet, I will humbly and shyly say this was not my message but *the* message of truth and love from an unconditionally loving God that was touching people. I can only imagine what it would be like if I could have told them the whole truth and nothing but the truth!

In order to relate to the youth, I would try to be as up-to-date as possible. I would use a new song heard on the radio and relate how the messages from the song were exactly the same as the messages of old that we have about God. I remember once using a song by the Thompson Twins called "Hold Me Now." The words begin, "I have a picture, pinned to my wall. An image of you and of me and we're laughing, we're loving it all." So many teenagers (let alone adults) have no concept of what it means to be unconditionally loved. Most of the New Age beliefs hold this principle and are not laden down with guilts or shoulds, "bad, bad, bad!" I wanted the "kids" at least to hear from their God what they couldn't get from society, peers or possibly their parents. God says, "You are something special, so special that I have a picture of you on 'my walls,' etched on my heart." The prophet Isaiah does say, "See, upon the palms of my hands I have written your name; your walls are ever before me" (Isaiah 49:16). You wouldn't hear many youths of the church say they know about that passage or live by its truth. But when they hear that message through the modern songs they hear on the radio, their ears perk up! Adolescents have enough to worry about and don't need a priest or church telling them they are bad if they do this or do that. I wanted them to know they lived in a New Age. I think they saw their parents laden down with a lot of "shoulds" or "have to's" and they didn't find it a very pretty picture to pattern their lives after. I felt the messages from the New Age about healing, unconditional love, seeing the face of God in one another, and in themselves, was much friendlier territory.

Now some of you may be asking, "Didn't you feel bad? Didn't you feel guilty? Did you feel deep in your soul that you were believing in something the church really didn't?" My answer is no. I really didn't have any trouble with the fact that these New Age beliefs were not professed by the church. And I didn't feel any of those emotions just mentioned. There was a deep, peaceful calmness in my acceptance of these truths. What saddened, or really probably angered me, was the fact that I couldn't openly talk about these new wonderful ways of understanding God, ourselves and our relationship with each other. I wanted to talk about channeling, a new way to connect with God and Spirit; I wanted to tell someone in the hospital about new forms of healing that were not just limited to the traditional; I wanted to give so many people not only new hope, but quite possibly new health and life; I wanted to let a frustrated, hurting, angry person in the confessional know about past lives or that others have also walked in their shoes (or vice versa); I wanted to prevent the need to hurt or be hurt by another, to sin or not sin against their sister or brother. I wanted the youth to know that they didn't have to look forward to a life filled with criticism, cynicism and hell. I wanted to tell them that there are modes and manners of expressing God even beyond organized religions and that they can have more tools to help them not only survive in the world, but thrive. I wanted to shout from the pulpit everything about my new-found journeys and relationship with God . . . but I couldn't. The gag order stood. My dad used to say, "You knew the rules of the ball game before you got in it. You can't change them now!" That is exactly the issue. This is the crossroads at which I found myself. My soul said all I have experienced is truth and the horizon to which we all should be directing our lives. I believed the back yards of the church opened up to these horizons, yet I felt locked out by the church, organized religions, who tend to say, "Don't cross that line."

The innocent outlook I held when I entered into the seminary was becoming blurred and restrictive. What more could pull me off center? I felt the gag order in place. Could there be something that would make me feel as though my hands were tied behind my back? Of course, I wouldn't be where I am today if it wasn't for one more thing to take me out of the loop, so to speak. And it wasn't one more thing, it was *one more person.* I'm not speaking about the person at my last parish who wrote a letter to the bishop about my offering the Blood of Christ (the wine, offered at communion) to the lay people. Too petty. Although it bothered me when someone, almost like a private detective, would delve into my past; that didn't push me over the edge. But I did wonder how that person failed to hear Jesus' message about "judge not, lest ye be judged" or "love one another as you loved yourself." The change (or should I say chains) wasn't about hearing that a priest back stabbed another priest again. (I was flabbergasted when one priest went behind my/our back(s) to tell the Bishop that we had a support meeting for kindred-spirited priests. That "brother" forgot the old adage about those living in glass houses ... .) Yes, I could feel the air being sucked right out of my stomach as I sat across from a brother priest at a meal and listened to him slash and cut away the lives of not only his brother priests, but slander and slur certain people in his parish community. No, it wasn't people writing letters to the Bishop, priests trampling over other priests, or backroom politics within the hierarchy of the church. It was the intimate dealings with one person. Intimacy. Relationship. Love of another.

Everyone knows the rules: no marriage, no intimacy, no love-making, no playing around. Although I knew some of the priests were so "human" despite their outward protestations. One minute they would be loving, caring, caressing *and even intimate*. The next minute, the next morning, they would be espousing the belief that they had stepped beyond normal, healthy practices and should reform their lives and call upon the mercy of the Lord. The rules say no, no, no! *But I was lonely*!

My first Christmas Eve of my priesthood at Sacred Heart was a glimpse of a greater, deeper feeling I would have in the future. I had just finished the Christmas Eve Mass and was calling the Mortons in Redwood City (a super supportive family from my seminary days at Menlo Park). I remember crying and saying to Rita, "I feel so-o-o lonely up here in my room all alone. Everyone's gone home and I miss my family."

Sunday afternoons were the hardest. There were a lot of couples out in public, walking on the beach, holding hands, doing things together. Some week nights were just as bad. When the meetings were finished, when the last client was seen, when the youth group had gone home, "Who you gonna call?" I wouldn't have survived as long as I did if it were not for my (few) close priest friends. Sometimes at 8:30, 9 or 10 p.m., we would get together for coffee, a glass of wine or a movie. Most of us were tired but at least we made the effort. One of the greatest message of the New Age movement that I came to believe is that we came down here, we chose to be "in skins" on earth, to relate, to love others and especially to love one person in particular. To love another in the relationship sense. Hands free and untied, to hold another's hand. And although I believe we all, with few exceptions, are called to be in relationships, I shall shift the focus to me. I felt I needed to be "in relationship" with another to experience the greater me.

So I began to put a prayer out to God, that if a relationship is what was meant for me, then may I find someone I could relate to on an equal spiritual level. Whoever God sends, may this person be open to a nonrestrictive understanding of God and our life with God. I loved serving the truth as a priest but I think God wants more for me than this. This gets into the whole subject of celibacy. I will say here and now that I don't agree with the current belief that priests should not get married. It wasn't that way for the first 500 years of the church. Many of our Popes were married as well as the first disciples. There were political, economical, as well as spiritual reasons why the church changed that rule. On the economic front, in the Middle Ages, the church was very much into property rights. Consider what would happen if the husband/priest died. Where would the property go? Right to the wife ... not to the church. Cut out the wife and everything remains copacetic. Spiritually, the church had good reason to think that when there is no family around the priest would then have more time to devote to God and the people. That may have been understandable in hectic times during the Middle Ages, but to continue that thinking today would be an affront to the hard working ministers of other faiths who allow their clergy to marry (and be women!). The celibacy discussion can go on and on. Be that as it may, I put forth here that I believed that God wanted something more for me. A companion in spirit as well as in intimacy. I wanted a partner, an equal, to be able to stand by me as I talked of healing in new ways; as I shared with others how they could be a channel for God; when I gathered in spirit with Native Americans; after I performed wedding celebrations. I believed I had the divine right, even after my call from God to the Catholic priesthood, to sit on a beach and hold my beloved in my arms while watching a sunset; to cry with a lover over the passing of a loved one; to dance; to travel; to sing; to love as any two people in love would do. I also came to a point in my life where I knew that to love another, on all levels, was to help facilitate my own growth and love of myself. I did not consider such thoughts sacrilegious. The Age of the Innocent was not over!

The next chapter is about the greatest gift God has ever imagined. As Saint Paul said so well and will echo for all eternity: "Love ... love is eternal ... love does not come to an end."

> *Be loving enough to God,*
> *to open your eyes and heart to new horizons.*
> *Be loving enough to yourself*
> *to trust your divinity and abilities*
> *to follow your sacred path.*
> *Be loving enough to others*
> *to draw to yourself one*
> *who will love you back*
> *and show you the love of*
> *and the face of God.*

Chapter Nine:
The Final Horizon
"Beauty and the Prince"

The first time I remember seeing her was like a blur. I knew someone special had just entered the room, but there was so much going on in my mind and in my sights, that I was not really able to focus on her beauty. It was October 31, 1993, Halloween of all dates! I was out on the floor doing the country western line dance and she was coming to the party with a gentleman friend. God does have quite a sense of humor, doesn't she? I had been working very hard all these past years in the New Age areas to uncover all the masks I'd been wearing which prevented me from seeing who I really was. Now that I had put out the prayer to find my companion, and now that God had seemed to place this answer before me, why was I wearing a mask?

I have always loved Halloween. It falls on the day before the feast day of All Saints. This used to be a holy day of obligation. My translation of a holy day of obligation was a day which presented itself to Catholics to once again remind themselves of ways through which they could deepen their relationship with God. Kind of a day off from all the mental gymnastics we all go through in the work world. This day was particularly fun for me in that we often had the kids come in their favorite saints costumes. Eventually, I would encourage them to come in their Halloween costumes, much to the chagrin of some of the "old timers." One of my predominant messages at these celebrations was, despite how much fun Halloween was, it was now time to take off our masks and be the saints on Earth that we were all called to be. If they/I thought we had fun with our masks on for Halloween, try taking them off and seeing how much fun life can be when we are our true selves.

Yet, here I was about to meet the love of my life and I was wearing a mask! When I finally did take it off, I didn't immediately connect with her. I was still in my Father Pat mode, trying to stay in contact with everyone in the room, being the eternal pleaser and care taker. And from what I understand, her first thought was, "Gee, that's Father Pat! I pictured 'Father' as a bald, fat, old priest!" No wonder we didn't connect right at first.

We had both come to Seattle for a conference on Spirituality in Business. Jacque Snyder and the Sacred Life Association had put together this conference in a magical setting outside Seattle in the deep forests under the majestic Mt. Si, in North Bend. It was a very conducive, spiritual environment for us to gather. This beautiful, natural setting exemplified the oneness of God with nature, all things and all people. We were there to gather with other like-minded people who believed that the business place could be "married to" spirit. Many practices were represented: teachers, computer experts, doctors, movie producers, scientists, body builders and many more. Oddly enough, I was there to represent spirituality in the churches, and in particular, the Catholic church. Strange isn't it, that you would have to point out how the church is spiritual. Wouldn't you take that for granted? I guess you and many others can answer that for yourselves.

When it came time for my talk, I slipped out of my normal garb, blue jeans and tee-shirt, and put on my official clerical clothes I wore to special occasions. I didn't do this for show or shock value. Many there already knew my story and my participation in the New Age areas. But many didn't. In others' presentations, I had heard stories of those who were hurt by the church, or who had moved beyond the church for other reasons. There were also Jewish participants who didn't understand the church. I wanted my presence to represent (by my collar?) that I was still a part of the official church and was proud of it. Yet, by being there, I had expanded my understandings beyond the traditional belief systems.

I felt very much at home with these people, even knowing that some of them had bitter feelings about the church. For some reason, I felt safer among these people for I knew that they would not be like some of the cynical, complaining, letter-writing people I had crossed in the church. The setting also brought me much peace. As I sat in the audience waiting to be called up, I could look out the window onto a beautifully dense, wooden forest of green. The sun shined on a teepee in the middle of the lawn. The rain had stopped and there was a glistening of water and light on the evergreens. I felt at home.

Jacque was giving the introduction from the front lectern. "So at this time, we present Father Pat McNamara, a Roman Catholic priest, who will be talking to you about Spirit and religion."

"Good afternoon! I am so happy to be here with all of you. First of all, I want to officially apologize to any of you, especially the Native American representatives, who have been hurt in some form or another by the church, a priest or a nun. I, in the name of the past, say I am sorry. The reasons for the wrong or hurt are buried in the past and no longer matter. You are now here in a greater understanding of God and love. I ask that you now let go of the past and forgive the church. The time is now and we have much to accomplish to bring the Kingdom of God about on earth."

Some were smiling, some crying. All seemed to be very accepting of me, my collar, and my position in the church. I next said,

> I think it was Karl Marx who said, "Religion is the opiate of the masses." Put in a more horrific way: religion kills the soul, dulls the senses, keeps the mask on, makes us the living dead.

After saying that, an old fear reared its ugly head. "What will these people think as I say such condemning words about the church? Surely one of them will stand up any minute and yell, 'Heresy! What gives you the right to say such things? What seminary did you go to?'" But no one did. I could tell their hearts were open. I could even see some of them shaking their heads in agreement as though they, too, were in the process of awakening their souls. So I continued,

Now, isn't that a nice way to start off the talk about organized religion? Boy, I bet the Bishop would be proud of me! But in a sense, you can see how non-Catholics and even more so non-Christians think this about the church. If you look at the Catholic church in particular and look at our sacraments ... and remember a sacrament is an outward manifestation of God, *i.e.*, God is present ... if you look at a few of these, you can see what is killing the people off. Take confession. "You're bad! You're bad! You're bad and you can't get close to God unless you purify yourself ... *and!* we will tell you exactly how you are to purify yourself." In the sacrament of baptism, we tell these young parents that their baby is stained with sin and must be cleansed or it won't get to heaven! I'm sure you have heard of the last rites. Wow, what a trip! If you have been bad all your life, bad to the bone, then your family can call on a priest at the last moment and anoint you with the holy oil and your sins will be forgiven. You can go to heaven, directly to heaven, without passing jail. That's telling the people that God hasn't been with them until just the end. Then there is the sacrament of holy communion, God's presence, God's nourishment, through the bread of life ... BUUUUT only if you are in a state of grace. And I'll tell you a lot of Catholics think they are not in the state of grace 'cause I see a lot of them sitting back during communion and not coming up to be nourished by God. Gee Whiz, you can see how people think organized religions cut you off from life and God. First, they tell you you are a wonderful creation from God and then they tell you how bad you are and how much you have to work to get back to God.

I felt I was on a roll. I was speaking from my heart what I had heard so many searching, frustrated or ex-Catholics say about their own pain. But I also believed that I had to balance this out with the good I believed was in the church.

But all that I just mentioned, can be seen as misconceptions of our religion. I *also* am a part of a church that I think has marvelous potential and offers wonderful gifts. I have sat in the confessional and have seen years of guilt and shame melt away just by sharing with the people the truths we have learned about a loving God and a companion brother named Jesus. I tell them there are many other angels and guides who are here to help us remember who we are.

I went on to give numerous examples of how the church could be of help, through other ways of kindness and compassion ... at healing Masses, meditations after communion, at times when people were dying, during baptisms and on and on. I shared with them a vision I saw in a shamanic dream mediation.

I was on a shamanic journey once and I found myself in the middle of a huge cavern. It was like the Pirates of Caribbean ride in Disneyland because the cavern was strewn with mounds and mounds of treasures. I thought I was in heaven! In the middle of this cavern was a ladder that caught my attention. It was going up to the ceiling. And when I climbed to the top of this ladder and opened the trap door, it came out to the altar in the middle of the church. I know this was telling me that there is so much spiritual wealth in the church that is not being tapped into and will not be tapped into until *we* avail it to ourselves. We must become the captain of the ship, so to speak. You can go to your church, your synagog, your temple and be raised octaves in your relationship with God, if you tap into the goodness and not the junk.

As I spoke now, there was no fear, no looking over my shoulder. This is how free and unbound I wanted to feel in the church on a daily basis, but couldn't. I wanted to be a light keeper in a lighthouse. I felt I was called to show people what wonderful seas they had to explore, and that they could leave the safety of their harbors, the church. Yes, there would be rocks and storms to avoid or navigate through, but there was help. The New Age horizons have so many treasures and I only hoped that I could help show the people where they were stored. I hoped I could guide them along the "trade-wind routes," so to speak, which would bring them to a fantasy island filled with ancient wonder and unbelievable futures. I explained this to the people in this way:

A few days ago, I was leaving San Francisco to come up here to this conference. The morning was just a miraculous day for me. It was about 7 a.m., as I was heading out to San Francisco from Marin County across the Bay. It was a clear day and to the west of me, I could see the full moon setting into the Pacific. To the east of me was a brilliant red sky waiting for the break of dawn to bring new life to the city of Saint Francis. Just before I got to the Golden Gate Bridge, I was able to pull over to the lookout point that used to be an old battery for the military to protect the opening of the bay. There was a sense of peace and tranquillity as I climbed to the top of the lookout to see the entire city across the bridge. People were quietly taking pictures of the setting moon and soon turned around in anticipation of the new sun about to make its appearance.

In the midst of this majestic scene, I had a message come to me about my talk on organized religion and how it relates to our conference. You see, I was standing on an ancient bluff encased with old bastions that used to sit there in all their glory, witnessing to the new explorers as they entered a harbor in search of new riches and adventures. And I had the feeling that that is exactly where we are today with regard to religion, with regard to science, with regard to medicine, business, *etc., etc., etc.* We are on the horizon of new adventures in Spirit. We all have our old bastions and military embattlements, our traditional religious foundations that are just that, foundations. But a new day is dawning and the Beauty of days gone by is now setting on the horizon. We can take the gifts we have been given and forge ahead ... or we can become stagnant and over grown and overburdened by the vegetation of old.

As I stood there and watched a massive freighter pass under the bridge and head out to unknown seas, I thought of us: as Catholics, other Christians, Jews, Muslims and Pagans. I thought of the awesome task ahead of us. We, like the explorers of old, come with a wealth of resources from the old lands, from the home lands, and we are ready to share our gifts and make use of our talents as we enter a new age. We also come with a new sense, unlike the explorers of old. We come with an openness and an unquenchable thirst to learn and grow, to explore new horizons and become more of Who We Are and Can Be. And, we come in equality to share all of that with others.

To empower the people is, and was, all I asked to be able to do. The freedom to express these thoughts was exhilarating. I felt like a new man, no longer burdened and beast-like. I could tell the truth of my message radiated out through my eyes to an open-hearted people. The gag rule was off. I could speak as a free person. Yet, my hands still felt bound. In my heart there was a lonely spot. I scanned the crowd as I shared my own love for them. Then, as my eyes moved from left to right, I found them stopping in the third row. I saw two eyes filled with such strong love and compassion. It seemed as though a glow, a bright aura, shone about this woman. Those eyes were connected with a beautiful woman with blond hair cascading down her shoulders. I knew she was the one I saw in a blur at the dance. I had met her briefly at the beginning of the conference. But for some reason, this time, our eyes locked on in an uncanny way for one brief moment. The people began to applaud at the end of my talk. I seemed to float back to my seat, not only because of the acceptance of my message, but because I had somehow connected with the eyes with this Beauty. I saw her stand up as the leader called the next speaker, Colleen Anderson. She was to speak on spirituality in the business field.

My total attention was focused on her. What elegance and charm this woman spoke with. Love was her center. Love is how she advanced through the ranks. Love is why no one was able to walk over her in a traditionally male-dominated world. I then heard her say, "And I too have to hold my place in my world, just as I am sure Father Pat has to hold his place in the church." At that moment, our eyes met again. I felt as though our hearts and souls connected on some deeper level. We remembered something very special about our lives. And on some distant cloud "out there," the angels rejoiced.

I remember seeing her at the end of that weekend as we were leaving the conference. She was walking up the driveway with the lush, rich, green forest behind her. Her Beauty equalled that of all God's nature. Without even knowing why, I asked her if I could take her picture. (I hadn't done that with any of the other people there ... all the rest of my pictures were of nature!) When I returned to San Diego and had the pictures developed, my heart began to soar as I saw her again.

I did see her two days after the conference, at a group channeling session with Zarathustra. It was funny because, again, she was with her gentleman friend. When the session started, I looked over to the couch where I had placed my jacket to reserve my spot. Sure enough, Colleen and her friend were on the same couch. I sat down next to her. She said, "Oh hi! It's nice to see you again," and introduced me to her friend. During the session, I started to feel this strange, never-felt-before energy in my heart. It felt like someone was turning up a strong electrical current within my chest. My mind was going over time, wondering what the heck was happening. This inner feeling produced a broad, boyish grin on my face. We talked a little bit during the session about what questions we should ask Z. But nothing special or intimate was said.

At the end of the session, we said our good-byes and she told me that she was moving from Tennessee out to California, near where I lived in San Diego. I said, "Great! Let's get together when you move in." I then remember moving away from her and going immediately over to Jacque, who knew me pretty well by then. I excitedly explained to her about this wondrous feeling that was going on inside and asked, "What's going on?" She got this cat-like grin on her face and simply said, "Just trust, Patrick. Just trust God." And then she walked away!

It took a month or two for Colleen to move all her

belongings out to California. Although I tucked the incident away in my mind, I do remember thinking about her once in a while. But I know I had not sorted anything out yet, because I had not told either of my two best-friend priest buddies about my feelings. I felt another surge of energy rush through me when I had a message in my mail box at the rectory that Colleen had called and could I please return her call.

So, our friendship began to grow. She invited me out to dinner and a movie with Paula and Mikey, her best friends. I also saw her at the classes Jacque and Z would put on in San Diego, as well as when Alex would come into town for healings. One Saturday afternoon Jacque asked that I rush over to help with praying over people before they went in to see Alex. I was so happy to see that Colleen was at the same "station" praying over people too. I was there in my collar and was for some reason feeling a little off-center. But when I saw her there and felt her centeredness, I calmed down almost immediately. Later that night after all the people had gone and the crew was about to eat dinner, I sat down on the couch to rest a bit. She came over and put her hand on my chest. I think she was about to tell me how wonderful it was that I was there to assist in the healings. My mind started to get jumbled and again wondered what was going on! She must have been able to tap into that because she said, "Whoa, why is your chest so tight? You need to let someone in to take care of you?"

"Oh no!" raced my mind. "She's got me figured out already!" She could see inside me: that I was vulnerable, frustrated and lonely. Could she be the one who was the answer to my prayers? Not only was she stunning in her physical appearance, she had an inner intuition and strength that was so keen. Hmmm, I'd better go out to some more movies with her and see what this is all about.

We soon found ourselves becoming very good friends, sharing ideas on Spirit, family and God. One gorgeous evening on the beach, while watching the sun set into the

Pacific, we completely opened ourselves up and shared our visions of the need for relationships in our lives to help make our work in life easier. Colleen remembers my grabbing her hand as we walked down some steep rocks. I held her hand intentionally longer than need be. She wondered silently what was going on and thought she had better let go before I got the wrong impression! What stuck in my mind that night was that I told her I would love to find that special, right person who would come into my life and bring stability to my Spiritual path and all the craziness I experienced in the priesthood. When we parted that night, I knew that I was starting to fall in serious "like" with her. All those teenage feelings and fears welled up inside of me. How am I going to let her know my feelings? Should I give her a light good-night kiss on the cheek? What if she didn't like me like that? As the grin on my face got bigger when I drove home that night, the butterflies in my stomach got stronger. Sounded like it was an excellent time to talk with my old therapist friend again!

Talking, communication and having a sound board are such wonderful tools. The best advice I was getting from my priest friends and therapist was to take it slowly and trust. Don't rush. Most of all, be honest. More and more, I was thinking about this Beauty in my life. She was such a bright light, not only in my life, but to so many of her friends, family and co-workers. She believed she came down to this earth to be a ray of sunshine. And although she sometimes had to face strong storms, she always came out shining and helped others see that love and light were the way.

I was starting to find more and more excuses to see her. One time she told me that she and a friend were meeting Jacque at the mesas in Northern Arizona to help some of the Native Americans. They were leaving on a Thursday morning and staying the whole weekend. Weekend! Yeeks, free weekends and priesthood don't go too well together. So I had to tell her I couldn't go. But by now my mind was working double over-time and I figured out that I could go with them and some how get back in time for work and Mass at the convalescent home with the "raisinettes" (well, they do have quite a few wrinkles at that stage in their lives) the next day! So I met her at the airport as a surprise. In fact, in trying to surprise her, I stealthfully walked passed her in the waiting area and then plopped right down into her lap. She looked up with a look of astonishment on her face saying, "Oh, Father Pat! I thought you couldn't get away from work!" I got up and I told her the time off would be short lived. I would have to make an immediate turn-around and be back in time for the "raisinettes" Mass the next day!

Since there were several of us on this leg of the trip, we had to rent two cars. Much to my dismay, Colleen was travelling in the other car. But we stopped several hours outside the mesas in the dead of night. The woman I was travelling with kind of knew about my feelings for Colleen so I suggested that we switch passengers. We all stood outside our cars for a moment. The stars were out. Colleen and I leaned up against one car and gazed out into the galaxies. I wanted to hold her hand and hug her so badly but wasn't sure how she would respond. I said, "Gee, wouldn't it be great if one day we could be out here looking at the stars and not stand here like 'stick people?'" Later she told me that the intention behind that statement flew right over her head. "Stick people?" she thought. "What's he talking about?"

That night, after we met up with our friends in the hotel, I needed a few minutes rest before I headed back to Phoenix again. At her invitation, I lay down on the bed next to her and placed my head on her chest. As I did so, I felt as if I was back in the arms of an eternal, celestial lover. The one I had dreamed of. The one for whom I had prayed to God. On the television in the hotel room, the movie, *South Pacific*, was playing. The words to "Some Enchanted Evening" were floating throughout the room.

*"You may see a stranger across a crowded room.
And somehow you know, you know even then,
that somewhere you'll see her again and again.
Who can explain it? Who can tell you why?
Fools give you reasons, wise men never try."*

But ... How cruel life could be at moments. I had to get up in a few minutes. We hugged and said our good byes. On the way back to the airport, I had this wide smile on my face and could see her Beauty in my vision. I pulled off the road in the early hours of the morning. Every star sparkled like a precious diamond in God's universe. I wondered if she was thinking of me. The energy I first felt when we sat on the couch back in Seattle had now turned into a soft, warm, peaceful glow throughout my body. I felt connected to my God and to all that I looked up to. But now there was a new connection to a Beauty-filled woman, "out there" on another of God's horizon.

As time unfolded, we began to share more of our intimate feelings for each other. A great intensity of emotions arose. Needless to say, we talked much about how this new relationship would affect my ministry. It was almost as though I knew my "lifetimes" of priestly ministry were coming to an end. I was honest in telling this Beauty that I was willing to trust and take the risk that I could move beyond my role as priest in the Catholic Church. She talked about how her personal solitary life would have to expand and grow to accommodate this new man in her life. Both areas would be a challenge for us.

I thought my transition would be hard for two reasons. First of all, there would be talk amongst the "brothers" in the priesthood. Sure enough, rumors started in priest-support groups that the liberal one, Pat, had a girlfriend and was taking her to the weddings he was performing. As usual with rumors, nothing could be further from the truth. I had come to have a deep love and respect for my Beauty and I would do nothing to compromise that by causing public scandal while still in the active ministry.

Because of these rumors, I decided after much prayer and discernment to go talk with the Bishop and let him know that I had fallen in love. The angels must have been with me in force that day. The meeting went like butter melting in my hands and it was concluded, with full consent and support of the Bishop, that I take time off to explore this relationship. I knew each of our higher selves, our souls, Beauty's, mine and probably the Bishop's, were smiling.

The second reason was equally challenging to integrate into our lives. You see, God knows that we are to continue to expand our horizons as humans, as God in skins. It is up to us to make that choice to move, to grow, to journey on. The hardest thing for this priest, now taking time to lay down the collar and explore new horizons, was to accept the reality of new territory "out there." Priesthood is a most interesting life. It is structured. You get up and say Mass. You know when the next meeting is, what liturgical season, such as Lent or Advent, is approaching and what needs to be planned out. To go from that structured life-style into one of rest and contemplation of what is to happen next requires an enormous amount of trust. I knew I was called to find greater ways to share the good news of God with others. The how, what and where were the unknown.

At my last Mass on Labor Day, I asked the people to contemplate new ways, nonlaboring ways, of resting in the truth that they, that we, are at "Home," now, with God, as co-creators on this planet. I was going to sing the song, "Bring Him Home," from *Les Miserables,* changing the words to ask, in prayer form, that God bring them "Home," on earth, now. As I prepared for that final Mass in quiet reflection in the sacristy, I closed my eyes and saw my whole life in the priesthood flash before me ... the retreats, the weddings, the Masses, the baptisms, the funerals, the joys, tears and laughter ... all in a matter of seconds. I could feel tears streaming down my face. Not only were there hard times during those years, but there was much joy. I was proud to be a part of all of that. And yet, I knew, just as a teenager knows when moving out of home for the first time, that I would miss a part of that history.

I felt a calming presence sweep over me as though the angels were there saying it was okay to move on. Much had been accomplished in the past, much more was to be achieved in the future. Beauty, my father, sister and brother-in-law and my faithful friend, Jen, were waiting outside the church after my last Mass. I felt their love and support. As we looked westward, we saw a most magnificent sunset. Again, there was a bit of sadness in my heart. Fifteen years in the priesthood is quite an investment, quite a pathway left behind. But as the huge, orange sun set in the deep blue ocean, I heard a whisper in my ear, undoubtedly from Joshua, that tomorrow is a new dawn, a new day, with a new Beauty.

We set the date of our wedding ceremony one year from the night we heard "Some Enchanted Evening" on the mesas. I, especially, wanted this to be a "public," so to speak, ceremony so that as many friends and family could witness the new-found love for the Beauty who had helped awaken me to new horizons of God. I was honored that her family, mostly Mormon, would grace us with their presence. My father and Colleen's mother were to be the official witnesses of the marriage. Many of her 32 nieces and nephews were a part of the celebration wedding party.

A light brightened and I saw her at the edge of the garden, ready to walk down the aisle in a beautiful, elegant wedding dress. Before the ceremony began, I sang a duet with Lonna to my Beauty. "I Have A Love" and "One Hand, One Heart" from *West Side Story* aptly summed up my intentions for the day. Her Prince, as she now called me, awaited her before the ministers: a tall, dignified West Indian from Trinadad, in colorful flowing robes; a black-

haired woman surrounded by white light; and a gentle-
manly, handsome, middle-aged priest, dressed in that
familiar black outfit with the small white collar, grinning
from ear to ear, with his heart aglow. Beauty, as well as
many others of us, could see the angels in their invisible
clothes, singing to God on high that destiny had been ful-
filled. Each person there to witness this union, made in
heaven, was opening their own heart to experience the
newness and wonderfulness of God through relationships.

I felt so alive. I met her eyes as she approached me. I
flashed back to that first moment I saw her in the audience
at the spirituality conference. I understood now why God
and spirituality had played and will continue to play, such
an important part in our lives. Like God touching the hand
of Man on Michaelangelo's fresco painting in the Sistine
Chapel, she touched my hand as we climbed the platform
and stood beneath an archway of flowers.

Her father, an Elder in The Church of Jesus Christ of
Latter-day Saints, gave a heart-warming welcome and in-
vocation. We had several inspirational readings, even one
from *The Velveteen Rabbit* about being real and in love. But
one reading by Paula really rang true in my heart:

> *Love is the secret symphony,*
> *The silver link, the silken tie,*
> *Which heart to heart and mind to mind*
> *In body and in soul can bind.*
>
> *We are all born for love;*
> *it is the principle of existence and its only end.*
>
> *And when love speaks,*
> *the voice of all the Gods*
> *makes heaven drowsy with the harmony.*

Love, as told by the seers of old,
comes as a butterfly tipped with gold;
Flutters and flies in sunlit skies,
weaving round hearts that were one time cold.

One word frees us all from the weight and pain of life.
That word is Love.

Hearing those words reminded me that I had been granted, I had discovered, this precious gift of love to spend eternity entwined, spirit to spirit, mind to mind, heart to heart.

I then spoke my vows of love and commitment to her heart and soul. The *Beast*, the part of me which had not experienced the fullness of Who I Am, was now a man in all the Spiritual wonderment of that word. I now was able to share my love for another, for my Beauty, emotionally, physically and Spiritually. I was thankful that she was so loving and accepting of my love for her. No longer was I sitting in the dark, lonely room of the rectory feeling gagged and bound. I was entwined in the arms of my beloved, passionately kissing her as I heard one of the ministers say,

"I now present to you, Beauty and her Prince."

This story, this true story, is to be continued for all of us!

Wedding

Post Script ...
Growth Scripts

"Speed Bumps in the New World"

The last chapter was a reality, I believe, blessed by God, watched over by angels, and followed through from the roots of my own higher self. I have never been happier in all my life. I have never felt closer to God and my love for all people at whatever stage of life they live.

You may have felt that the chapter reflected only the bad times in the priesthood. In no way do I want to say that the experiences I had as a priest were all bad. Nothing would be further from the truth. I had many great, moving, happy, joy-filled moments during my priesthood. But, I felt like I was stagnating and was compelled to move on, move beyond and out into a greater play ground of God.

After I decided to leave the active Catholic priesthood, I chose to become licensed by the state as an ordained minister. I had, and still do have, a deep desire to serve God and the people of God. I set up a business called **Sacred Moments ✧ Sacred Events**. I want to be there for people at times of celebration in their lives, be it at marriages, baptisms or funerals to name a few celebrations. In my brochures, I told people how I had "moved beyond the Roman Catholic institution into a greater ministry for all." I again wanted to assist in making their life-celebrations *sacred* *events.* This is especially true if they no longer were able to celebrate these events in their particular organized religion, for whatever reason, be it divorced, remarried, alienated, or fallen away. I mailed brochures about **Sacred Moments ✧ Sacred Events** out to people on my Christmas mailing list and to those whom I had kept abreast of my transitions. Sure enough, the Bishop's office called a few weeks later and the chancellor had to tell me he was "disturbed" by my brochure. He feared people would still consider me a Catholic priest (which I told him I would thoroughly explain that I was not). Then he honed in on the part about "moving beyond." He was "disturbed" because it sounded as though I was abandoning ship! I am not sure he heard me when I told him I still loved the church. I just felt the necessity to move beyond ... not necessarily to greener pastures, for much of what the church has to offer is great. But, I think we need to allow ourselves to make the choice to gaze over the hill, so to speak. That is no condemnation of the pasture from which we left. Nor would it be a condemnation of the shepherd for starting his flock off originally in a particular area. But please, no guilt or shame heaped upon us when we want to nourish ourselves in new and exciting ways that allow us to continue to move onward and outward!

Another sad postscript is an unsigned note I received in the mail. It was typed on plain paper, very similar to the kind of note a priest I know used to type back and forth to me. All it said was:

"Thank God, you are really, finally gone!"

For a few moments, I felt as though I had been hit with a ton of bricks. I allowed this to slip me back into "hell," in terms of Teotihuacan. I wanted to judge and I felt judged. I was tempted to feel like the bad boy because I judged. On the other hand, I felt like the codependent child who doesn't want to offend others. But after talking with my angels, heavenly and earthbound, I quickly recovered. Some people, even some priests, feel very threatened by the possibility of new realities out there beyond their comfort horizons. In the same way, so too would a second grader be scared to think that there is even a possibility of high school in the future. My task is not to respond back in kind, but to move on, stay centered, and send only light and love. On the lighter side, maybe it was a message from Spirit saying (of course, again, without judgment!), **"Thank God you finally really have moved on!"** Bravo!

One last lesson ... knowing they will never stop. The day of our wedding rehearsal, I received a call from someone who worked at a rectory and was planning on coming to the wedding. There was fear in this person's voice as they said that there had been a message placed with the answering service from a man, whom this person thought was another priest: "Don't even think of going to that wedding ceremony tomorrow!" I felt a sadness that fear had to be used in such an ugly way! The next day there was an extra empty chair at the wedding. How sad ... they missed a magical, mystical celebration!

This postscript *will* end on a happy note. God is so good, especially when you can see God through a wider window. Go to the mountaintop, as did Jesus for transfiguration, as Martin Luther King did for his vision. Become more enlightened to the overall plan, the dream of God. You are a part of the dream. You are the dreamer as well. If you are currently in an organized religion ... God bless you for honoring your choice to be there. But don't forget to open your eyes and look beyond the walls so to enhance your life, your adventure. Every postscript in your life, be it at the end of a day, an event, a relationship, a moment ... every postscript should be signed with a shining gold star. God is your director of all events. You are here on this earth plane to excel, to adventure, to have fun. Look around yourself. See the Beauty and paradise that God created. Enjoy it. Go for it! Break on through to the other side!

Suggested Reading

Brinkley, Dannion. *Saved By The Light.* New York: HarperPaperbacks, 1994.

Cannon, Dolores. *Between Death and Life.* Ozark Mountain Publishing, 1995.

Cannon, Dolores. *Jesus and The Essenes.* England: Gateway Books, 1992.

Cannon, Dolores. *They Walked with Jesus.* England: Gateway Books, 1994.

Carey, Ken. *The Starseed Transmissions.* New York: HarperSanFrancisco, 1982.

Carey, Ken. *Vision.* New York: HarperSanFrancisco, 1985.

Carey, Ken. *The Third Millennium.* New York: HarperSanFrancisco, 1991.

Millman, Dan. *Way of The Peaceful Warrior.* Tiburon: HJ Kramer Inc, 1980.

Millman, Dan. *Sacred Journey of The Peaceful Warrior.* Tiburon: HJ Kramer Inc, 1991.

Moody, Jr., M.D., Raymond A. *Life After Life.* New York: Bantam Books, 1975.

Moody, Jr., M.D., Raymond A. *Coming Back: A Psychiatrist Explores Past-Life Journeys.* New York: Bantam Books, 1990.

Rampa, T. Lobsang. *The Third Eye.* New York: Ballantine Books, 1956.

Roman, Sanaya and Duane Packer. *Opening To Channel— How To Connect with Your Guide.* Tiburon: HJ Kramer Inc, 1987.

Walsch, Neale Donald. *Conversations with God—An Uncommon Dialogue*. New York: G.P. Putnam's Sons, 1995.

Weiss, M.D., Brian. *Many Lives, Many Masters*. New York: Simon & Schuster Inc, 1988.

Weiss, M.D., Brian. *Through Time into Healing*. New York: Simon & Schuster Inc, 1992 (with Forward by Dr. Raymond Moody).

About the Author

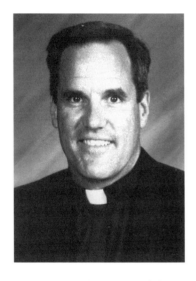

Patrick McNamara,M.A. served as a Roman Catholic Priest for the Diocese of San Diego from 1980 to 1995 in a variety of positions including Associate Pastor, Youth Minister, High School Campus Minister and Religion teacher. He received his Masters in Counseling Psychology at Santa Clara University in 1989, and performed his Counseling Internship at the Christian Institute for Psychotherapy and Training in San Diego. In 1979, Patrick received his Masters in Divinity from St. Patrick's Seminary, Menlo Park, Ca. A Juris Doctorate in law was granted from University of San Diego School of Law in 1975. Patrick attended undergraduate school at the University of Washington (1968-1972) and recieved a B.S. in Psychology.

Patrick is currently living in Cardiff, California with his wife, Colleen, the love of his life. He continues his ministry of touching people with the truth of God through various avenues. He is a licensed minister and performs weddings and other celebrations with *Sacred Moments ❖ Sacred Events.* As a spiritual counselor, he offers guidance through *Sacred Pathways ... an adventure in Self Discovery.* Patrick also remains steadfast in his commitment to be in union with spirit through *Sacred Moments with Joshua.*

If you wish to communicate with Patrick about his book or his life's work, you may contact him at the following address or phone number. (Please enclose a self-addressed stamped envelope for his reply, if corresponding via mail.)

Patrick McNamara
1657 Andorre Glen ❖ Escondido, Ca. 92029
(760) 741-9273
e-mail: Furpat@aol.com

Other Ozark Mountain
Books you might enjoy:
(Books by Dolores Cannon)

Conversations with Nostradamus, Volume I
Conversations with Nostradamus, Volume II
Conversations with Nostradamus, Volume III
Between Death and Life
Jesus and the Essenes
Keepers of the Garden
A Soul Remembers Hiroshima
The Legend of Starcrash
They Walked with Jesus
Legacy from the Stars

Conversations with Nostradamus is available
in abridged form on audio tape cassette.

For more information about any
of the above titles, write to:

OZARK
M O U N T A I N
PUBLISHERS

P.O. Box 754
Huntsville, AR 72740-0754

or call

1-800-935-0045

Wholesale Inquiries Welcome